The Efficient Golfer

90⁰

120⁰

60⁰

Using Videotape, Measurement and Good Sense
To Improve Your Swing and Putting Mechanics

Robert Anthony Prichard

somax

Illustrations by Gary Crumpler.

Illustration model Joe Dolby.

Cover and book design by Danil Zorin.

cal activity, check with your personal physician before performing any of the tests, drills or exercises in this book. The author and publisher disclaim any responsibility for any injury or other consequences from following the contents this book. Any slights of people, places or organizations are unintentional. Drawings are not representations of persons living or dead, unless they are specifically named in the text.

Publisher's Cataloging-in-Publication Data

Prichard, Robert Anthony.
The efficient golfer : using videotape, measurement and good sense to improve your swing and putting mechanics / Robert Anthony Prichard.
p. cm.
ISBN-13: 978-0-9792102-0-4
ISBN-10: 0-9792102-0-8
CCN 2006911037

1. Golf--Study and teaching.   I. Title.

GV962.5.P75 2007   796.352'3
                          QBI06-600720

Published by Somax Sports Corporation, 4 Tara Hill Road, Tiburon, CA 94920

www.the-efficient-golfer.com   www.somaxsports.com

License Agreement

Purchaser agrees, by purchasing this book, that all the methods of measurement and analysis, analogies, illustrations, drills and exercises described in this book are the property of Somax Sports Corporation and the author Robert Anthony Prichard.

Purchaser agrees that he or she is buying a license to use the methods of measurement and analysis, analogies, illustrations, drills and exercises in this book only for his or her own use and that of his or her own immediate family, limited to parents, siblings, spouse and children.

Purchaser agrees not to use any of the methods of measurement and analysis, analogies, illustrations, drills or exercises in this book for commercial or educational purposes without the express written permission of Somax Sports Corporation and the author Robert Anthony Prichard.

No excerpts or reprints of any part of this book may be published by mechanical or electronic means without the written permission of Somax Sports Corporation and the author Robert Anthony Prichard.

Purchaser agrees that monetary damages may not provide a remedy in the event of a breach of this agreement, and therefore, Somax Sports Corporation has the right to enforce this agreement by means of injunction without the necessity of obtaining any form of bond or assurance whatsoever.

This agreement shall be governed by and construed in accordance with the laws of the State of California. Any controversy or claim arising out of or relating to this agreement or any alleged breach of this agreement, shall be arbitrated in accordance with the rules of the American Arbitration Association in San Francisco, California. The award shall be binding upon the parties and judgment may be entered in any court have competent jurisdiction. If any arbitration or action at law or in equity is brought by either party arising from, concerning, or to enforce, or interpret this agreement, the prevailing party shall be entitled to reasonable attorney's fees, costs and necessary disbursements, in addition to any other relief to which such party may be entitled.

If purchaser does want to be bound by this agreement, return the unread book immediately to the seller for full refund.

Anyone coming into possession of this book agrees to be bound by the terms of this license agreement.

Table of Contents

Introduction

The modern conventional golf swing is a combination of new ideas superimposed on top of centuries-old traditions.

It is time for some new thinking.

Our background is in science. We look upon the golf swing as an engineering disaster passed along from one generation to the next.

It is time for a fresh perspective.

We need a new analysis of the golf swing.

Putting is no different. As practiced today, it is an amalgam of new ideas and old traditions. This is why so many skilled players miss short putts. Conventional putting and conventional putters can almost guarantee that you will turn birdies into par, or worse.

It is time for a new analysis of putting.

Engineers applying general scientific proceedures have produced great strides in golf equipment. We apply the same engineering principles to the swing, the putt and the golfer.

Re-engineering the golfer is the key to shooting lower scores.

The reason that average golf scores have not improved is that everyone has ignored the physical characteristics of the golfer. The most important piece of equipment on the course is body of the golfer. Measuring and improving your strength and flexibility in golf-specific ranges will make the biggest improvements in your game. It's just a matter of knowing how to do it.

This book is a paradigm shift in golf. It has some quick tips, but they won't do you as much good as changing the whole system. If you are willing to change, this book will show you the way.

CHAPTER ONE

Can We Measure Efficiency?

Efficiency simply means the maximum results with the least effort.

Efficiency means accuracy, distance and consistency with the least amount of effort.

Can we measure efficiency? Isn't it just a matter of opinion?

It is not. We **can** measure efficiency in the golf swing. We apply the same method of analysis that has produced 44 Gold Medals and 11 World Records for our elite athletes.

Efficiency is a result of **RSSSA** (pronounced Russia).

Range
Sequence
Separation
Speed
Alignment

These five characteristics tell us how efficient an athlete is in any sport. We will measure these characteristics in the golf swing to show you what an efficient swing and putting stoke looks like.

As you improve your efficiency, you will feel a new ease in your swing and putting stroke. You will have more success getting the ball to your target. You will drain more putts with fewer strokes.

Efficiency means lower scores with less effort.

CHAPTER TWO

Range = Distance

The Rocket Theory of Golf

When you swing a golf club, you are essentially putting the clubhead into an orbit around your body. The clubhead then hits the golf ball, sending it into a short orbit around the earth.

A satellite is usually put into orbit with a multi-stage rocket.

A golfer is a five-stage rocket. Stage One is the legs; Stage Two the hips; Stage Three the trunk; Stage Four the arms, and Stage Five the hands.

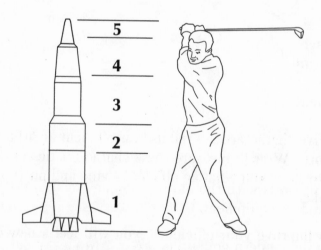

The golfer as a five-stage rocket.

This analogy clears up a lot of problems in analyzing the golf swing, and helps us to identify the most efficient possible swing for golf.

Fuel

Rockets have fuel. The mistake that golfers make is that they think that their 'fuel' is their muscles.

It is not. It is their Range.

Your Range is how far you turn away from the ball.

The more you turn away, the more fuel you have to power your downswing.

Here are the Ranges of a golfer who won more PGA tournaments than any golfer in history. Here is his 'fuel'.

A golfer with Range like this drove an average of 280 yards with the old persimmon woods. With modern equipment, that would be over 300 yards.

Here is the modern golfer who has thrown away most of his fuel by restricting his Range—all in the hope of being more accurate.

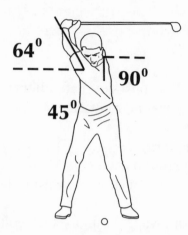

This is the modern golfer restricting his Range, hoping to be more accurate. There can be a short-term benefit from restricting your Range, but only if it improves your Alignment. But Range and Alignment are separate issues. It is much better to improve both your Range and Alignment if you want to avoid injury and disappointment. Restricting your Range often leads to injury.

When you discard the fuel that comes from Range, you have to make up for it in order to maintain your club head speed. What do you use?

You use muscular effort.

If our modern, restricted-backswing golfer wants to hit 280-300 yard drives, he has to rely on muscular effort.

Which means he has to lift weights to build up his strength.

Which means he will get stiffer, because lifting weights tears muscle fibers.

As any Sportsmedicine physician or scientist will confirm,

you get stronger when you lift weights because you tear the individual fibers in your muscles (there are thousands of fibers in each muscle).

Your muscle fibers repair by forming scar tissue (that's much of what makes your muscles look bigger) and bigger fibers, which increases your strength. Of course, you also form microfibers (another form of scar tissue) in the connective tissue membranes that surround each muscle, and these microfibers make you stiffer.

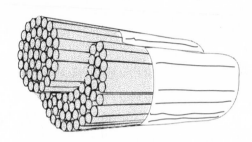

This is a model of your muscles and connective tissue. Each muscle (shaded area) is composed of thousands of individual muscle fibers. Each muscle is surrounded by a thin membrane of connective tissue called fascia. These membranes allow the muscles to slide past each other, which they have to do in order to stretch or contract. When you injure a muscle, microfibers form between the surrounding membranes in order to immobilize the area so that it can heal. Microfibers are nature's internal cast. Unfortunately, once the muscles have healed, the microfibers not only do not go away, they tend to accumulate over time, making you stiffer as you get older.

Once formed, microfibers will continue to accumulate over time, making you stiffer year by year, even if you stop lifting weights. These microfibers cannot be stretched out. The way to release them is with Microfiber Reduction (see Chapter 12).

Most of the work we have done with our professional golfers is releasing microfibers created by lifting weights and/or doing 'core' work (sit-ups, crunches, etc.).

Even our young pros in their twenties have lost Range and flexibility because they started lifting weights and doing 'core' work in their teens.

As you get stiffer, what happens?

You reduce your Range even further. To make up for this loss of Range, you have to really torque your body on your downswing to get any club head speed at all. When you do this, you greatly increase the stresses on your whole body, but especially your lower back and shoulders.

The short backswing has spawned a new industry: treating the shoulders and backs of golfers. Of course, they are treating the symptom (shoulder and low back pain) and not the cause (restricted turn, lifting weights). Our program for fixing low back pain is found in Chapter Eleven (Low Back Pain).

If big muscles are the key to long drives, how does a 125 lb. LPGA player average 275 yards on her drives? The answer is Range: how far she turns away from the ball.

For 280-yard drives, without effort, we recommend minimum Ranges of 60° of hip rotation, 120° of trunk rotation and 90° of arm rotation, which looks like this

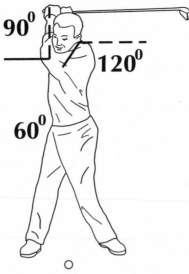

These are the minimum Ranges for an efficient, effortless backswing. The minimums are 60⁰ of hip rotation, 120⁰ of trunk rotation and 90⁰ of arm rotation.

When you couple these Ranges with efficient Sequence and Separation and sufficient hip Speed, you can hit 280-yard drives without effort.

This is what we mean by efficient—without effort.

With sufficient flexibility (Chapter 8), you can make a 60/120/90 backswing without any feelings of tension. You only need tension in your backswing when you lack flexibility.

The human body is not a spring. You do not coil up with tension and then violently uncoil. The tension you feel on your backswing is your opposing muscles trying to overcome your own stiffness. If you are not stiff, you will feel relaxed.

Tension is not good for golf. You want to have a full turn, but feel loose and relaxed.

No effort.

Measuring your Range

Set your camcorder on a tripod in front of you. Set the shutter speed to 1/1000th of a second, or 'sport' mode. Turn the camcorder on and take three or four swings, preferably with a ball teed up. Play the tape back on your TV with frame-advance until you are at the top of your backswing. Now measure your Ranges.

> Always use an erasable marker on your glass TV or plasma screen. Do not use any marker on an LCD screen, as it may stain it. If your screen is plastic, find someone who has a glass TV or plasma screen.

You will have to guess your hip Range. Use the illustrations in this book as a guide.

You measure your shoulder Range by drawing a horizontal line from your right shoulder and a line connecting your two shoulders, just as we have done in the illustrations above. If you turn less than 90°, you just have to guess.

You measure your arm Range by drawing a horizontal line from your left shoulder, and another line through your upper arm, as we have done in the illustrations above. If your left upper arm is below horizontal, record your arm Range as a negative number.

If you don't have 60°, 120° and 90° Ranges, then you are either restricting your turn or you have flexibility problems. Go to Chapter Eight (Are You Flexible Enough for Golf?) to learn how to measure your flexibility.

Is it possible to hit accurate drives with a 60/120/90 turn?

Of course it is. All you need is good Alignment (Chapter 6).

Range = Distance.

Alignment = Accuracy.

It's important to keep these two aspects of the swing separate. Don't try to increase Accuracy by restricting Range. You improve accuracy by improving Alignment (Chapter 6).

If you have found that restricting your Range has improved your accuracy, it is only because you have inadvertently improved your Alignment, not because you have shortened your backswing. Again, it is critical that you understand that Range and Alignment are different are two completely different aspects of the golf swing.

Can increasing your Range really increase your distance?

One of our pros increased his longest drive on tour from 295 to 400 after we increased his Range. Another pro increased his average drive from 280 to over 300 by increasing his Range.

Remember, efficient means without effort. Effort makes golf, or any other sport, worse.

You know you don't play your best golf when you try harder.

Why not make the game easier by increasing your Range?

CHAPTER THREE

Sequence = Consistency + Distance

Sequence is the second aspect of efficiency we analyze after Range.

Sequence is the order in which you fire your stages (legs, hips, trunk, arms, and hands) during your downswing.

The Rocket Theory of Golf (Again)

When you swing the club, you are basically placing the club head in orbit around your body.

The usual way to put an object into orbit to use a rocket.

Rockets have stages. The stages are fired in sequence, from the ground up.

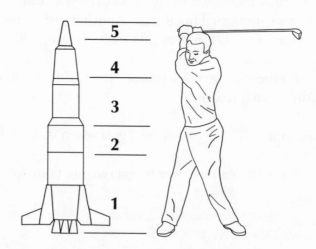

As we said before, a golfer is a five-stage rocket: legs, hips, trunk, arms and hands.

Most golfers fire Stage Five (the hands) first. You can tell Stage Five has been fired because the clubhead moves vertically at the beginning of the downswing. Other golfers start their downswing by sliding or shifting their hips (Stage Two) to their left. Some start by rotating their shoulders (Stage Three) first. Some fire all five stages at the same time (oops!).

This is why very few launch engineers at Cape Kennedy are recruited from the ranks of golfers!

There is only one way to get a satellite efficiently into orbit, and that is to fire the stages in sequence from the ground up.

The same is true in golf. Any Sequence other than Stages 1-5 is inefficient.

You may have also noticed that rockets are not shifted to the right and then to the left on the launch pad prior to firing. This is because launch engineers and rocket designers decided long ago that it would add nothing to the accuracy of the launch, and would, in fact, make it worse.

The same is true of the golf swing. Any weight shift to the right or left prior to impact will make your swing less accurate.

Analyzing Your Sequence

An efficient downswing starts with the left knee, followed by the left hip, the left shoulder, the left arm and the hands. If you put adhesive tape on your left knee, left hip, and left shoulder, videotape your swing from the front with the camera shutter at 1,000th of a second, play the tape on your TV, go to the top of your backswing, pause the tape, draw ellipses with an erasable marker around the tapes on your left knee, left hip, left shoulder and circles around your hands and club head, and then advance the tape frame-by-frame, you can see the order in which you fire your stages.

Putting adhesive or duct tape on your lead knee, hip and shoulder will help you more accurately identify your downswing Sequence. Drawing ellipses around the tapes and circles around your hands and clubhead will tell you when they move.

You can tell when you fire Stages One-Three because the tapes will move to the right on the TV screen. Shifting your hips (Stage Two) is not the same as rotating your hips. Make sure that when your hip tape moves that you are turning your hips and not shifting or sliding them.

Your arms (Stage Four) will fire when your hands move to the left on the screen. You have fired your hands (Stage Five) when the clubhead moves vertically. If your clubhead only moves horizontally to the left, you are dragging it along with Stage four, but you have not yet fired Stage five.

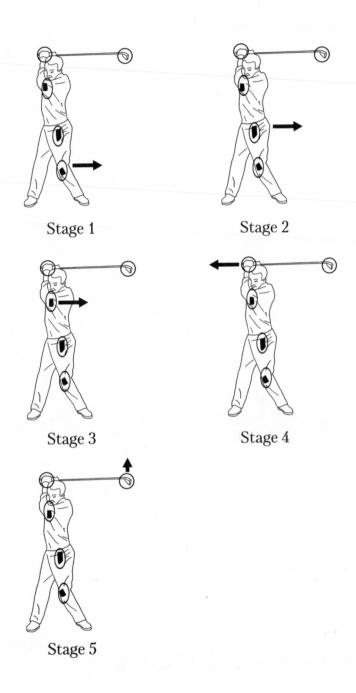

Stage 1

Stage 2

Stage 3

Stage 4

Stage 5

Watch for the tape, your hands, and club to move in the small ellipses and circles you have drawn on your TV screen. This will give you an accurate representation of your downswing sequence.

Write down your Sequence. It can be 1, 2, 3, 4, 5; or 5, 4, 3, 2, 1; or 2, 3, 4, 1, 5; or any other combination.

If you fire two or more stages at once, write the numbers above each other, like this

$$1$$
$$2, 3, 4, 5$$

Always keep track of your Sequence. It is the key to consistency.

Improving your Sequence

Stand in front of a mirror and go to the top of your backswing position. If you are inside, use five iron with a 20" shaft so that you don't damage the ceiling. Make sure there is no one around you. You don't want to clobber your roommates, spouse or kids.

Start your downswing with your left knee. Notice that as you move your left knee to your left, your left hip starts to move. Continue to rotate your hips to your left by pushing off the inside of your right foot. After you have turned your hips to your left, you will notice that your left shoulder starts to turn. Next, your arm will start to move and the club head will move horizontally.

This is your efficient Sequence. It is the only Sequence that is efficient. Anything else (shifting or sliding hips, starting with hips first, moving everything at once, starting with shoulders, arms or hands) is inefficient.

The best golfers in history have used this 1-5 Sequence. Five of the top seven golfers of all time had this sequence. They were good because they were consistent. They were consistent because they had an efficient Sequence.

Sequence = Consistency, just as Range = Distance and Alignment = Accuracy.

In an efficient 1-5 Sequence, the power generated by the legs (Stage One) is transmitted to the hips (Stage Two). The power of those two Stages is transmitted to the trunk (Stage Three). The combined power of the first three stages is then transmitted to the arms (Stage Four). Finally, the power of the first four Stages is transmitted to the hands (Stage Five), and finally to the club. This is how you get a club head to go from zero to 110+ mph in less than 1/3rd of a second (time of the downswing to impact) without effort.

This is how we get satellites into space. Exactly the same sequence.

No one has ever successfully launched a satellite with any other sequence.

What is your Sequence? How do you launch your clubhead? How do you launch your ball? What Sequence do you use?

If it is not 1-5, make sure that it is. With every club (except, of course, your putter).

Effort and Power

Efficient Sequence + Efficient Range = Effortless Power.

Poor Sequence + Restriction = Powerless Effort.

To generate Effortless Power, you need a new swing thought.

From now on, your swing thought for your downswing will be

LEFT KNEE. START WITH THE LEFT KNEE.

Most golfers waggle their club before they take their club back. This only reinforces the idea that you are swinging the club with your hands.

We recommend you waggle your left knee before you take your club back. This way, you remind yourself to start with the left knee (right knee if you play left-handed).

Starting your downswing with your left knee is the best way to insure an efficient sequence. Of course, it won't be easy until you have sufficient flexibility (Chapter Eight). If your body is glued together, it won't be easy to fire your Stages separately so that you have an efficient Sequence.

But once you have mastered this Sequence and combined it with a Range of 60, 120, 90, you will be able to hit 280-yard drives without effort. Your Range and Sequence will supply most of the fuel. The remainder will come from Separation and Speed.

There is one last aspect of Sequence we need to cover, and that is casting.

Cast Point

Here is a drawing of the Cast Point, when the arm is 45 degrees below horizontal, or when your hands are at your hips on your downswing.

This is the Cast Point. Your left arm is 45° below horizontal on your downswing.

Once you have moved your videotape to the Cast Point, draw a line through the center of your left arm and then draw another line at a right angle to that arm line. Your club shaft should be on or behind that 90-degree line. If it is ahead of that line, you are casting your club. If it is behind that line, you are lagging your club, or delaying the firing of Stage Five (the hands), which is even better.

This shows a golfer casting his club 30°. He is firing his hands too early, losing much of the speed he has generated with Stages 1-4.

This shows a golfer who is not casting his club.

This shows a golfer who is lagging his club. He
is delaying the firing of his hands (Stage Five).
If you can lag your club, you will get even more
distance.

Imagine if Stage Five of a rocket was fired before Stage Four
had fired. Stage Five (the smallest stage), with its tiny supply
of fuel, would separate from the rest of the rocket and quickly
fall to earth, taking the satellite with it:

Not a great way to get a satellite into orbit. Not a good way to
get a ball down the fairway. Make sure that at the Cast Point,
your club is on or behind the 90° line.

The Left Knee is the Key to Efficient Sequence and Consistency

Can something as simple as Sequence really make you a better golfer? Can it really be the key to consistency?

While we were teaching one of our pros to start his downswing with his left knee, we accompanied him to his club to videotape all his swings from the front as he played nine holes. We made notes on every shot. When we reviewed the tape later, we could see that he started some downswings with his left knee (Stage One), and others with his hips (Stage Two).

When he started with his left knee, he hit his intended target.

When he started with his hips, he did not.

Later we returned to the same course where he hit 20 balls onto the green with his nine iron. By this time he had mastered starting his downswing with his left knee (Stage One).

All the balls landed within six feet of the flag.

He said he had never been that consistent with any of his irons.

CHAPTER FOUR

Separation = Distance + Consistency

While watching a rocket launch, you probably noticed that the stages separated from each other as they fired.

The same is true in golf, but only if you have an efficient swing.

If you have an efficient downswing, your left knee will move, when you advance the videotape frame-by-frame, for one or two frames before your left hip moves. If your downswing is not efficient, they will both move together. The same is true with the subsequent Stages. Two frames of Separation between every Stage is your goal for an efficient downswing.

Firing two Stages at the same time is not a good idea for a rocket launch and is a poor strategy for launching a club head and golf ball into their orbits.

You want Separation between each and every Stage. One frame at least. Two frames are much better. Practice in front of a mirror. Move your left knee first. See how far you can move it before you move your hips. See how far you can move the left knee and hip before you rotate your shoulders. See how far you can rotate your shoulders before you move your arms. Finally, see how far you can more your arms without the club head moving vertically.

This is Separation. One frame of Separation is good; two frames are better.

The largest amount of Separation we have seen was three frames between Stage one and Stage two. This was a historically great golfer.

Separation is not possible if you are stiff. If you lack sufficient flexibility for golf (Chapter Eight), your Stages will move together. You won't have any choice in the matter.

Separation is not possible if you restrict your backswing. Everything is too bunched up. The modern, restricted backswing robs you of Separation. Restricting your backswing is like trying to go to the moon in a very short rocket where the stages don't separate.

Good luck! Send us a postcard when you get there!

Separation and a full backswing, on the other hand, will add explosive power to your drives, with absolutely no feeling of effort. It will seem as if you are doing nothing, but the ball explodes off the clubface.

Separation will also increase the consistency you get will an efficient downswing Sequence.

Once you have practiced Separation in front of a mirror, see if you can transfer this Separation to your swing. Videotape yourself hitting some balls. Make sure you have the adhesive tape markers on your left knee, hip and shoulder. See how many frames of Separation you can achieve between each Stage.

CHAPTER FIVE

Speed = Distance

The only aspect of efficiency where you need muscle strength is in the Speed department.

You need strength in the rotators of your hips, the one area where you don't have it,.

You don't need bigger muscles; your hip muscles are already big enough.

You need to learn how to recruit more of the individual muscle fibers in your hip muscles.

Strength is mostly a result of recruitment—how many fibers in each muscle that your brain fires or contracts. When you need less strength (handling an egg) you don't shrink down the size of your muscles, you just recruit fewer fibers. When you need more strength, you recruit more fibers.

Ninety percent of the increase in strength you get from lifting weights comes from recruitment. When you repeatedly lift a weight, you fatigue the fibers your brain habitually fires. It then hunts around for additional fibers to fire. Over time, you train your brain to fire more fibers.

Unfortunately, lifting weights tears also tears muscle fibers.

Fortunately, you can fatigue muscle fibers without tearing them. We will tell you how.

Testing your Strength

Here is a simple test. Lie on the floor on your stomach. Keeping your knees together, bend your knees 90 degrees so that the soles of your feet point straight up. Now move your feet away from each other, still keeping your knees together. Have someone hold your feet apart while you try to bring them together. Chances are very good that you cannot bring them together.

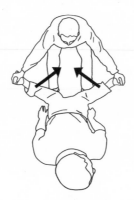

This is a simple test for hip rotator strength. Your helper should provide just enough resistance to make it difficult for you to bring your feet together. Don't overdo this test. You want to test your strength, not prove how strong you are. You don't want to hurt your knees. Check with your physician before you do this test.

If you hip muscles are strong, you should be able to easily overpower anyone holding your feet apart. I once did this test with a 22 year-old breastroker who threw me back ten feet across the room when she brought her feet together. She set a World Record in the breaststroke when she was 13, so of course her hip muscles were strong, as all the speed in breaststroke comes from the kick. When I have done this same test on senior male collegiate breastrokers, they could hardly budge their feet. They were using their adductor muscles for their kick, and thus were not very successful. She used the right muscles for the job.

Every golfer we have tested has failed this test. The reason is that there is no resistance to hip rotation in the downswing, so these muscles never get strong on their own.

Now compare the strength of your hip muscles to your paper-thin trunk muscles.

Sit on a stool with someone standing behind you. Turn your shoulders to your right. Have someone hold them in place while you turn back to center. Chances are good that you can easily do this.

Again, don't overdo it. Don't hold your breath. Your helper supplies just enough resistance to make it difficult for you to turn. Check with your physician before doing this test.

So, which muscles do you use to power your downswing? Do you use your larger, potentially stronger hip muscles, or your paper-thin trunk muscles?

Your trunk muscles, of course. This is why they are stronger than your hip muscles. You use them more often against resistance.

Muscles only get stronger when they have something to work against.

Your hip rotators, the biggest muscles in your body, have no natural resistance during your downswing, so they remain pitifully weak.

Your trunk muscles, on the other hand, work against the inertia of the club. They are paper-thin. They are your obliques, your stomach muscles. But with enough practice, you can recruit every last fiber in them.

Even if you lift weights, you will not have strong hip rotators. The reason is that weights do not strengthen the rotators of the hips. They strengthen the extensors and flexors. Not the rotators.

Increasing Your Strength and Speed

The only machine that strengthens the rotators is the Somax Power Hip Trainer (Chapter Fifteen--Training Aids and Equipment). The Power Hip Trainer will safely increase your strength. It has a sturdy metal spring at the base that provides just enough resistance so that you can fatigue your hip rotators without tearing them. It comes with a DVD that contains 26 drills for right and left-handers.

If you flunked the hip rotation strength test, consider a Power Hip Trainer. You may also want to get a Hip Speedometer (Chapter Fifteen--Training Aids and Equipment), so that you can transfer your new hip speed to the range and the course.

The Hip Speedometer is a pager-like device you clip on your belt. You turn it on, and before you take your swing, you press the record button. When you have finished your swing, you press the record button again, and the LCD shows you your maximum acceleration and deceleration. In this way, you get instant feedback on the heart of your swing—the rotation of your hips. It comes with a DVD that shows you how to use it, and some drills you can do with it. Nice way to improve your efficiency and distance.

You need Speed in your hips. For an efficient downswing, your hips need to be at least 45 open at your Cast Point, and 60 open just prior to impact in order to achieve a 280-yard drive without effort.

This is a golfer whose hips are 45 open at his Cast Point. You will be able to achieve this when you have sufficient hip speed for an efficient swing.

This is a golfer whose hips are 60° open at impact. You can only get here with sufficient hip speed and flexibility. This is your goal for an efficient swing that will produce 280-yard drives without effort.

The Wisdom of Throwing Your Weight Around

Why do you need to accelerate your hips? Because, as we all know from high school physics, Force = Mass X Acceleration. Your hips have a lot of mass. The faster you accelerate and decelerate them during your downswing, the more force you develop to power your club.

You can tell if you are accelerating your hips enough, because they will be 45° open at the Cast Point, and 60° open prior to impact.

You can tell if you are decelerating your hips, because they will stop at 60° open prior to impact, stay stopped until after impact, and then continue to turn.

You have hips. You might as well use them. If you have big hips, it's even better!

When your hip rotators are strong, it doesn't take any effort to turn your hips fast.

In addition to their mass, your hips have the potential to be three times stronger than your arms, just because of the size of your hip muscles. When athletes lift weights, they can usually press three times the weight with their legs and hips as they can bench press with their arms.

Why power your downswing with puny arm muscles? Pull out your big guns.

Want to get the ball down the fairway? Use your hips.

So get your Power Hip Trainer. Order a Hip Speedometer. Work on your hip rotation strength until you can snap your feet together, no matter who is holding them apart.

Then go out and impress your friends.

Swing Thought for the Hips

Just before you start your downswing think

LEFT KNEE. FAST HIPS.

Videotape your swing from the front. Measure your hip rotation at the Cast Point and at impact. Don't stop until you have reached your goal of 45/60.

Remember, you don't 'clear' the hips so the hands can come through. You don't play golf with your hands; you play golf with your hips (unless you are putting, in which case you putt with your stomach muscles).

In golf, as in the rest of life, the tail (hands) does not wag the dog (hips)—the dog (hips) wags the tail (hands).

Even great golfers 'think' they play with their hands.

If we played golf with our hands, we would play sitting down.

Golfers are great when they have great hips. The great ones have fast, intelligent hips. They just are not aware of it, because golf is 'hand—centric'. Just as we once thought the earth was the center of the universe, and that everything revolved around it, so golfers think that their hands are the center of the golf universe, and that everything revolves around their hands.

It's not true.

The fastest hips in golf belong to the best player in golf.

The fastest hips in boxing belonged to best boxer in history.

The fastest hips in baseball belong to the best batter in baseball.

Do you see a trend here?

Fast hips are a large component of 'talent'. The most 'talented' athletes have the fastest hips, the most success, and the biggest paychecks.

Increase your 'talent' by increasing your hip speed. Success and the paychecks will follow.

Everything in the golf swing revolves around the hips—not the hands.

This is the 21st century. It's time to change our ideas.

You don't believe sun and stars revolve around the earth, do you?

CHAPTER SIX

Alignment = Accuracy

The most accurate ballstriker of all time was the golf-ball hitting machine Iron Byron. Iron Byron hit 280-yard drives that all landed in a circle with a five-yard radius—all day long.

Iron Byron could do this, not because it was a machine, but because of the way it was designed.

Iron Byron was designed with constant Alignment. Its spine angles were constant, and its club, 'hand' and arm were always on plane.

If you want to improve your accuracy, you will do the same.

The conventional golf swing is a disaster of mis-alignment.

Let's see what actually happens.

Alignment Down the Line

Here is a golfer at address, with his swing plane drawn in, and his Spine Angle measured.

32^0

This is a conventional address position. Notice that the hands are dropped well below the swing plane. This is supposedly a 'relaxed' position, but is really a recipe for disaster.

Here is the same golfer at impact, with his Spine Angle measured again.

Our conventional golfer has changed his Spine Angle from 32° to 10° and his hands, arms and clubshaft are now on his swing plane.

Here is what a golf machine, or ball-striking robot, looks like at address and impact. We call our machine Super Striker. Notice that the two positions are identical.

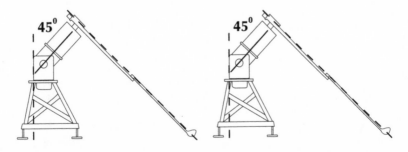

Super Striker has exactly the same position at

address and impact because of the way it was designed. If it were designed like a conventional golfer (hands dropped at address), it would have to change its Spine Angle between address and impact. Fortunately, it was not designed like a conventional golfer, or it would have been hitting balls all over the place.

Changing your Spine Angle between address and impact requires years of practice to make good ball contact. If you don't make the exact adjustment, and your Spine Angle at impact is off by only one degree, you will not hit the ball with the center of the clubface.

With his body parts (spine, arms and hands) wandering all over the planet between address and impact, it's a miracle that a golfer with a conventional address position can hit the ball at all.

Why do golfers set up with their hands dropped, and then change their Spine Angles during their swing?

Convention.

Starting with your hands dropped at address is purely a matter of convention.

Subsequently changing your Spine Angle is a matter of physics.

When you start with your hands dropped at address, you have to stand up at impact, because centrifugal force is pulling the club away from you, extending your arms and bringing your hands up to the swing plane. The club is traveling at 100+ mph and pulling with 100 lbs of force. This is the same force you experience picking up a 100 lb. sack of cement.

This pulling force extends the club head 6-7" beyond what it was at address.   If you don't stand up prior to impact, your club head will be 6-7" underground instead of striking the ball.

You can demonstrate this amount of extension during your downswing by standing at address with a ball teed up and your hands in their usual dropped position. Now, without changing your Spine Angle, extend your arms and club until they are in a straight line. Your club head will slide 6-7" past the ball. You have to compensate for this extension every time you swing. This is why golfers have to spend countless hours on the practice range, trying to make good ball contact.

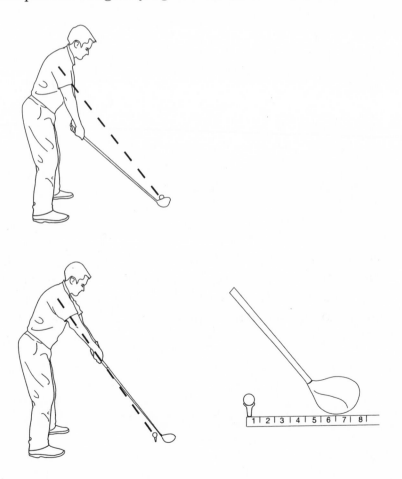

Some golfers have tried to solve the centrifugal force problem by gripping the driver so strongly that they do not allow their arms and club to extend at impact. Some of the golfers who have done this were the best golfers in history. They were very accurate ball strikers. But they all ended up with the yips (see Chapter Ten--The Yips).

What seemed like a good strategy at first, turned out to be a bad idea.

The other problem with dropping your hands at address is that you have to swing back under the swing plane.

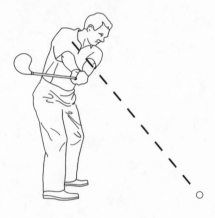

When you finally get to the top of your backswing, you have to re-route your club somewhere up behind your head (where you cannot possibly see what is going on) in order to get your club on your swing plane in preparation for your downswing.

So, if you want to improve your accuracy with your driver, woods, irons and wedges, put your hands on the swing plane at address and keep your hands and club on the swing plane during your backswing, downswing and follow through.

This is what Super Striker looks like down the line. Notice that its Alignment (Spine Angle, arm and club in relation to swing plane) is always the same.

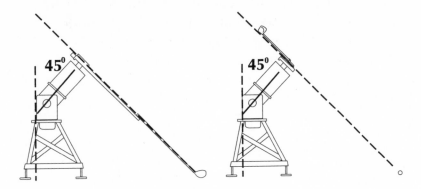

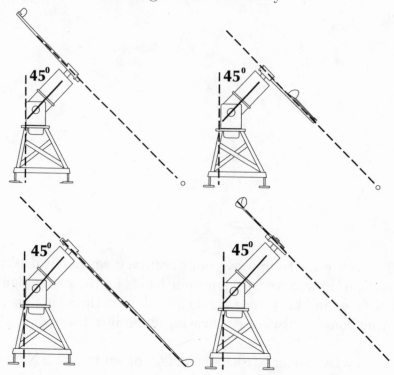

Super Striker has efficient Alignment. Its Spine Angle is always the same, and its arm and club are always on the swing plane. It hits the ball perfectly straight because of its design, not because it is a machine. Alignment creates accuracy.

Here is what a golfer looks like with efficient Alignment

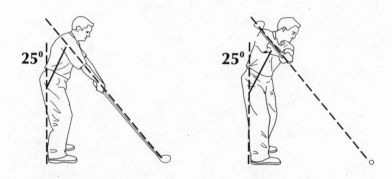

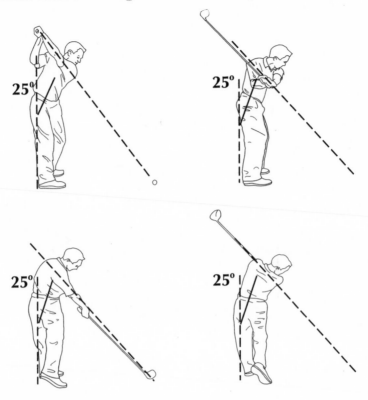

Design your swing to look like the most accurate ball striker of all time—and you will be more accurate. Good Alignment means accurate ball flight. Sloppy Alignment means spraying balls left and right and hitting them short because of poor ball contact.

Improving your Alignment will lower your score and reduce your practice time.

Front Alignment

Here is Super Striker from the front.

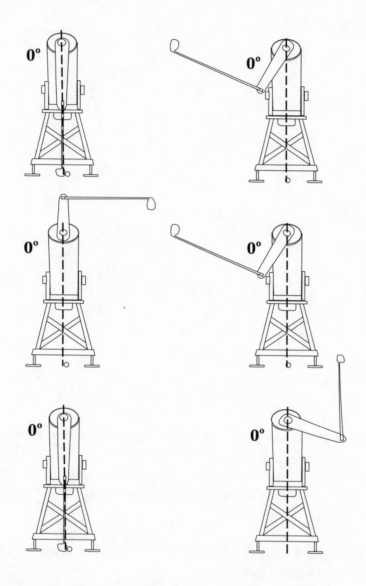

Notice that Super Striker's Front Spine Angle is exactly the same throughout its swing. Notice that it does not shift its weight. It does not 'load up its right leg'. It does not 'get its weight behind the ball'.

This is what a conventional golfer looks like.

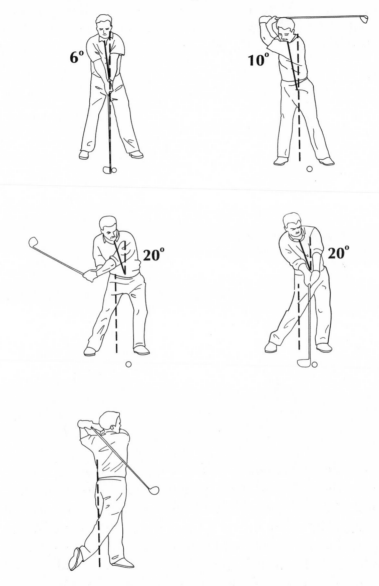

Notice that our conventional golfer shifted his weight to his right leg during his backswing, then he shifted his hips to his left during his downswing, and, as a result, his Front Spine Angle changed from 6° to 20°. This is a 333% change in his FrontSpine Angle from address to impact.

Imagine if Super Striker were designed to look like our conventional golfer, shifting Stages One and Two (legs and hips) to its left at downswing, with an increase in it Front Spine Angle.

We spoke before about a golfer being a five-stage rocket, launching the clubhead in an orbit around his body. Imagine if a rocket launch were designed to look like a conventional golf swing. The entire rocket would be shifted to its right just before the launch sequence. Then the first and second stages would be shifted to its left and the second stage would be fired first (starting the downswing with the hips). This is what it would look like.

The rocket, of course, would never get the satellite into orbit.

If Super Striker were designed to shift its weight and have a right spine tilt during the downswing and at impact (so that it looked like a human golfer), what would be the effect on its ball flight?

All its drives would go to the right.

You can demonstrate this for yourself.

Stand at address with your driver. Keep your hands and arms constant, but tilt your spine to your right.

Your clubface opens up. When you hit a drive with an open clubface, what happens?

Your ball goes into the right rough.

Weight Shift

Nearly every golfer on this planet shifts his weight to his right leg on his backswing, and then starts his downswing by shifting his weight toward his left leg. It feels 'natural'. Golfers have done it for centuries.

Everyone seems to agree that you 'have to get your weight behind the ball' and 'shift your hips toward the target'. But Super Striker does not get its 'weight behind the ball', or 'load up its right leg', or 'shift its hips toward the target" yet it can hit balls 280 yards into a 30-foot circle all day long. If it was shifting and bending like a conventional golfer, do you think it would be as accurate?

No.

Super Striker is designed to keep its weight 'over' the ball. If you want more accurate shots, you will do the same.

When you weight shift, you have to change your Front Spine Angle. You have no choice in the matter. Once you get your weight on your right leg during your backswing, you commit yourself to poor alignment at impact. This one move commits you to 'army golf'—drives that go 'right, left, right, left, etc.'.

Shifting weight prior to impact is the fastest way to turn a great golfer into a good golfer.

Shifting your weight prior to impact will sentence you to years of frustration and disappointment.

When your clubface opens from increasing your Front Spine Angle, you have to turn the clubface with your hands to square it up again. You have only 9/30ths of a second (less than 1/3rd of a second) from the top of your backswing to impact. It is likely that you will have to make the needed correction in the last third of your downswing, or in less than 1/10th of a second.

Sometimes you are lucky, and your drive goes straight.

Sometimes you fail to square it up, and the ball goes right.

If you turn your clubface too much, you will hook the ball.

Are you willing to base your success in golf on your ability to square up your clubface in less than 1/10th of a second while your clubhead is traveling at 100+ miles an hour?

Do you like living dangerously?

Do you like to bet the house on a weak hand?

Weight shift is why golfers spray their drives all over the course.

They look befuddled when their drives go right and left, because they feel that they are doing everything 'right' by 'keeping their weight behind the ball'. They don't realize that doing things 'right' makes everything wrong.

So, stop shifting, and just turn. It looks like this.

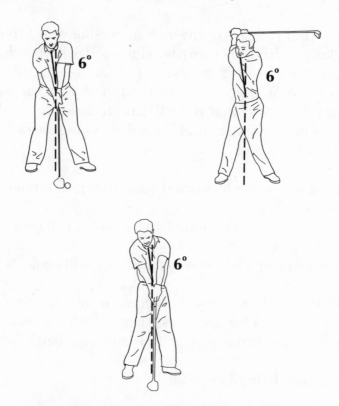

Here is a golfer who has improved his Alignment by refusing to shift his weight prior to impact. By going against convention, he has improved his chances of hitting the ball straight. By eliminating weight shift, he can now keep his Front Spine Angle constant, which will mean his clubface will be square at impact.

After impact, you can shift your weight to your left leg. The ball won't care. It's already long gone.

After impact, you can allow all your weight to shift to your left leg. Your ball will be going straight toward its target, and you can relax and enjoy watching it.

Hitting the Ball Straight

To improve your accuracy, you need to improve your Alignment. You can improve your Alignment with four simple steps.

1.Put your hands on your swing plane at address with all your clubs.

2. Keep your hands and club on your swing plane during the backswing, top of backswing, downswing, impact and follow through

3. Keep your Spine Angles, front and down the line, constant

4. Don't shift your weight to your right or left prior to impact. Keep your hips between your heels until after you have sent the ball on its way. Prior to impact, always keep your weight over the ball.

Can it really be this simple?

It is. When you are setting up at address, think to yourself:

"I AM SUPER STRIKER".

No more bobbing up and down, no more weaving right and

left. Golf is not boxing.

No more fighting centrifugal force. Let the force be with you.

Constant Spine Angles.

No weight shift prior to impact.

Stay on plane.

Too simple.

Once all your drives land in a 30-foot circle, 280 yards out, then you can work on your fade and draw.

Measuring Your Alignment

You don't want to try to improve your Alignment by feel.

'Feel' is highly overrated in golf.

You don't want to design your golf swing by 'feel'.

At the beginning of the last century, airplanes were designed by 'feel'.

The fatality rate for the first pilots was extremely high.

As airplane designers relied more and more on measurement, planes became faster, safer, and could fly longer distances.

If you don't want to crash and burn on the golf course, design your swing by measuring your Alignment.

If you want your shots to land on target, measure your Alignment.

Here's how.

Measuring Down the Line

Address

Start with your address position on the tape of your swing from down the line. Draw in your swing plane by drawing a line from your shoulder to the ball, and extend this line back behind you. Make sure you use an erasable maker, and draw only on a screen that is glass. Do not draw on a plastic screen, such as found on LCD displays.

Do not erase this line until you have completed your analysis. You will need this line to see where your club and hands are during your entire swing.

Next, draw a vertical line up from your heel, and a line through the center of your trunk. Measure your Spine Angle.

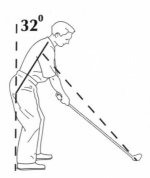

Write down all your angles. In this way, as you remeasure, you will be able to measure your progress.

Backswing

Advance the tape frame-by-frame and notice if your hands and club are on plane. It is likely they are not, and your swing will look like this.

For an efficient swing, you want your hands and club on plane, like this.

Top of Backswing

Your left arm should be on your swing plane line if you have efficient Alignment.

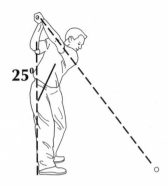

If your clubshaft is horizontal and on plane at the top of your backswing, you will not be able to see it. Your hands will cover it.

Measure your Spine Angle at the top of your backswing. Write it down and compare it to your Spine Angle at address. They should be the same.

Many golfers 'stand up' at the top of their backswing (Spine Angle becomes smaller) in order to get a bigger turn when they lack flexibility. It makes more sense to keep your Spine Angle the same as at address, and measure and improve your flexibility (Chapter 8).

Other golfers contract their stomach muscle and pull their head down (Spine Angle becomes bigger) in anticipation of 'muscling' their downswing. Relax your muscles and just turn away from the ball with a constant Spine Angle. A good backswing has no tension.

Downswing

Advance your tape so that you can see if your clubshaft and hands are on your swing plane during your downswing.

You want to have your hands and club on your swing plane.

Impact

Go to impact, and draw a line through the center of your trunk. Measure your Spine Angle again. Your Spine Angle should be the same as at address. If you dropped your hands at address, this will be impossible, unless you maintained your Wrist Angle, in which case you will develop the yips.

Follow Through

Advance the tape to follow through. Your clubshaft should be on your swing plane.

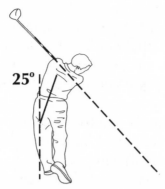

Every engineer records a 'baseline' measurement. It is the only objective way to evaluate progress. Take the same care measuring your swing as engineers did measuring the car you drive and plane you fly in. Your car and plane get you to your destination safely. A carefully measured and engineered swing will get your ball safely to its destination.

Measuring from the Front

Address

Cue up your tape to your address position from the front. Draw a vertical line up from the center of your two feet. It should go through your belt buckle. Draw a line from your belt buckle to the center of your shirt collar. Measure your Front Spine Angle. Write down your measurement.

Most pros have a Front Spine Angle of 3-11 degrees. You have to tilt your trunk and head to your right with a right-hand-low grip, but make your tilt as small as possible. Don't tilt to your right to 'get your weight behind the ball'.

Also, don't tee up your ball too far forward in your stance, or you will have to shift your weight to your left during your downswing. All ball-striking machines have their ball teed up just forward of the center of their stance. They hit 280-yard drives with no problem. You only need to tee up forward in your stance if you are going to shift your weight to your left leg prior to impact.

Top of Backswing

Go to the top of your backswing. Draw a vertical line through the center of your feet and another vertical line through the center of your trunk. Now draw a line through the center of your trunk to get your Front Spine Angle. Record your Front Spine Angle for the top of your backswing. Your Front Spine Angle at the top of your backswing should be the same as it is at address.

The center of your hips should be over the center of your feet. Make a note of where your hips are in relation to the center-line coming up from between your feet.

Impact

Hopefully, you have rotated your hips prior to impact, so you can't use your belt buckle to measure your Front Spine Angle at impact. Instead, draw a vertical line through the center of your hips and another line through the center of your trunk. Also, draw a vertical line through the center of your two feet. Now measure your Front Spine Angle.

Your Front Spine Angle should be the same as it was at address. Your hips should be centered between your feet, as you see here.

Another way to see how much you shift your weight prior to impact is to draw two vertical lines from the inside of your heels. If you don't shift your weight, your hips will stay within these two lines. If they move outside of the lines, you have shifted too much

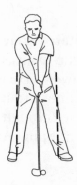

Making Improvements

As you work on keeping your hands on your swing plane at address and keeping your hips within your vertical heel lines prior to impact so that you can stay on plane and keep your spine angles constant, tape yourself again and again to measure your progress. Write down your new measurements and compare them to your starting point.

Don't rely on ball flight.

You only have control of one thing on the golf course, and that is your own body. As you improve your Alignment, your ball flight will get better. It may get worse at first as you will have many old habits to overcome, but it will get better.

Don't forget, you have made millions of swings with poor alignment. You may have made progress by now because you learned to compensate with your hands. Improving your alignment will mean giving up your compensations. This may take some time.

If you were racing a car with poor alignment, you would always have to compensate with your hands to keep the car on the racetrack. You have to do that now with your swing. But just as you can't win a race with a car with poor alignment, it is difficult to win a match or tournament with poor alignment.

Don't get discouraged. Keep working on your alignment and your ball flight will follow.

Alignment is the Key to Accuracy

Alignment is the horse that pulls the cart (ball flight). Don't put the cart before the horse.

Learn to love and appreciate good Alignment. It will make you a ballstriker that you can be proud of.

One of our pro golfers said, "Before improving my alignment, my best shots were a 7. Now they are a 10."

If you want help improving your Alignment, we can provide telephone coaching, Internet swing analysis, golf camps and individual programs. See Chapter Fourteen.

If you find that you just cannot improve your Alignment so that you look like Super Striker, you have flexibility problems. Read Chapter Eight and measure your flexibility.

Golfers with flexibility problems often think they have 'mental' problems. Because they are unaware of how stiff they are, or how many alignment problems they have, they feel that they don't hit the ball well because they don't 'concentrate'. We have found that golfers who think this way often successfully run one or more businesses while attending to their family and civic duties.

If you have problems improving your Alignment, don't blame your mind.

Measure your Alignment and flexibility.

CHAPTER SEVEN

Pendulum Putting

Everyone today says that they are 'pendulum putting'.

Are they?

The Stroke

This is what a modern conventional 'pendulum' putting stroke looks like.

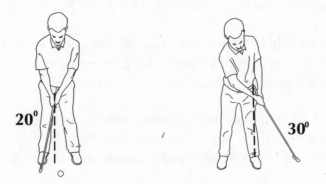

Do you know of any pendulum that swings 20 degrees in one direction and 30 degrees in the other?

Of course not.

And, by the way, this 'pendulum' pauses at the 30-degree end while the golfer admires (or bemoans) his putt.

No, this is not a pendulum, not by any stretch of the imagination.

This is what a genuine pendulum putt looks like.

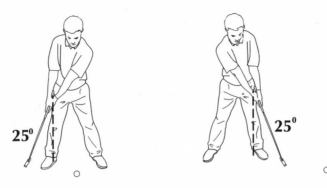

The number of degrees the putter goes back is exactly the same as the finish, just like a real pendulum.

And is this what a pendulum looks like from the side?

This is what a genuine pendulum looks like from the side. It hangs straight down.

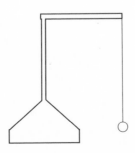

Do you see any resemblance between the 'pendulum putt' and a real pendulum?

We don't either.

Which is why we teach our golfers to putt like this.

This looks more like a real pendulum. The arms are hanging down and relaxed, instead of being sucked into the stomach, full of tension.

The Putter

But you can't let your arms hang down relaxed with a conventional putter, because it is too long.

Why are putters so long?

Convention.

Someone decided to make them about the same length as the short clubs.

It was a stupid decision that has been handed down from generation to generation.

A pendulum putter is shorter (around 30", depending on your

height), with a 79° lie angle so that your arms can hang down. The putter head weighs around 500 grams so that you can use the weight of the head instead of your muscles to putt the ball. It is center-shafted for balance and accuracy.

It is the putter that we designed to facilitate a pendulum motion. You can buy one (along with a DVD showing how to use it) from our website **www.somaxsports.com** See Chapter Fifteen (Training Aids and Equipment).

The Grip

A symmetrical, pendulum swing is easier if you have a symmetrical grip, which looks like this.

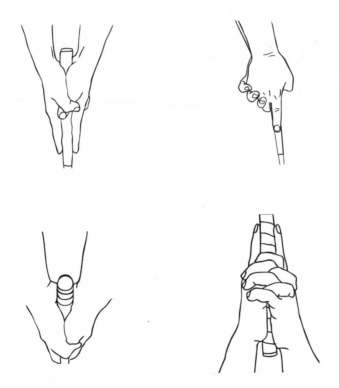

This grip is very stable. The putter grip rides in the little valley between the thumb and heel pads of your hands (almost as if they were designed to hold the putter this way) and along the insides of your extended index fingers. The interlocked thumbs and remaining three fingers provide the pressure to hold everything together in one unit.

The Stance

Do you take a narrow stance when you putt?

Why?

Isn't putting the only time you don't want your hips to move? Isn't a narrow stance inherently less stable than a wide stance? If you are not sure, try this little test. Have someone push your hips sideways in your conventional, narrow putting stance. Now, try the same test with your legs in a driver-width stance, your feet both slightly turned out. Notice how much more stable you are.

This is why we advocate a wide stance while putting. You want rock-solid, stable hips.

Why didn't someone think of this before?

They were too busy putting like their grandfathers.

The Putting Muscles

What muscles do you putt with? Your hands? Your arms? Your shoulders?

Not if you want an efficient putting stroke. For an efficient pendulum putt, you putt with your stomach muscles.

Again, there is an easy test. Have someone stand behind you while you putt. Have them place their thumbs and forefingers around your waist, applying some pressure to your obliques. As you bring your putter back, both of you should feel your right obliques contract. As you let your putter go, your muscles relax, and then you contract your left obliques.

For an efficient pendulum putt, use your stomach muscles to rotate your rib cage. Your shoulders, arms, hands and club go along for the ride. The putter head describes a soft arc, the face opening on the backswing, squaring up at impact, and closing at the finish.

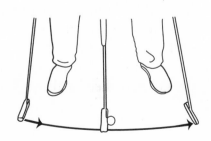

Keeping the putter face square and the putter on a straight line during the putt seems like a good idea, but it forces you to use your arm and shoulder muscles. The problem with using your arm and shoulder muscles is that these are the very muscles we tense up when we are under stress. You are probably aware that when you are under stress, you tense up your shoulders. This is why it always feels so good to have someone massage your upper back and shoulders, because we always tense up these muscles.

Can you putt well with tense muscles? If you tense up your shoulder muscles when under stress, and you have to make a pressure putt, do you want to have to rely on the very muscles you are tensing up to get the job done?

Wouldn't it make more sense to rely on muscles you do not habitually tense up, like your stomach muscles?

Of course it would. Which is why our golfers make more putts using their stomach muscles than when using their arm and shoulder muscles.

You will be amazed at how much more relaxed you feel putting when you switch from a straight line stroke (which forces you to use your arm and shoulder muscles) to a pendulum stroke that relies on your stomach muscles. You will also miss fewer putts.

The Finish

The compulsion to hold the putter at the end of the stroke can be eliminated by letting the putter fall back to the end of the backswing after putting, and then letting fall back to the impact position and letting it ground. Only then do you look up. This also helps keep the head still, which is critical to accurate putting.

The Spine

There is one more thing you need to be concerned about, and it is the most important part of putting.

But no one has ever seen it because you keep your shirt on when you putt.

Set up your camcorder behind you. Take off your shirt and putt some balls. It should be a fairly long putt (around 8' indoors). Now look at your tape. Look for the small bumps made by the individual posterior processes of your spine. You should be able to see a small amount of movement at every bump from the top of your shoulders to the top of your hips.

If you are like most golfers, you will see that the motion of your spine stops short of the bottom, or there are several vertebrae that move as a group instead of individually, or that your spine curves to your right or left.

All of these restrictions or deformities degrade your putting.

While your spine should move, your head and hips should not. Draw a semi-circle around your head and lines next to your hips to see if you have any motion there.

Your spine is the central axis of rotation when you putt. Any restriction is like having rust in the crankshaft of your engine and the drive train of your car. Having a bent spine is like having a bent drive shaft.

To give you an idea of the importance of free movement at every part of the spine during the putt, one of our pros went from #113 to #1 on tour in putting average after we released the microfibers that were restricting the movement of his spine.

CHAPTER EIGHT

Are You Flexible Enough for Golf?

The answer is no.

You are not flexible enough for golf.

Golf requires more flexibility than any other sport.

To find out if you are flexible enough for golf, record and measure these four ranges. These are the **minimum** ranges you need for an efficient swing (60, 120, 90 degree turn away from the ball).

Not the maximum.

The **minimum**.

Taking the Photos to Measure

The easiest way to record the first three ranges is to lie on the floor. Have someone get down on the floor with a camera or camcorder and record your ranges in the positions you see described below. For Trunk Rotation, have them sit in a chair facing you and photograph or videotape you from the front.

Internal Hip Rotation

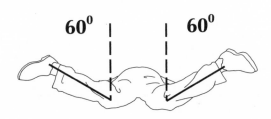

Lie on your stomach with your legs together. Keeping your knees together, bend them 90° so that the soles of your feet point toward the ceiling. Move your feet away from each other to form the V you see. On your photo or TV image, draw vertical lines up from each knee. Draw a line through the center of each lower leg. Measure the angle between this line and the vertical.

Neck Rotation

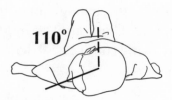

Lie on your back and turn your head to your left. Don't force it. You want to see your unrestricted range. On your photo or TV image, draw a vertical line through the center of your head. Draw a line through the center of your head and your nose. Measure this angle. Now repeat this entire process by turning your head to your right.

Arm Flexion

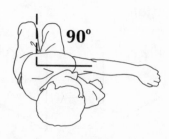

Lie on your back. Reach up to the ceiling with your left arm. Keep your elbow straight. Let your arm fall across your shoulders to your right. On your photo or TV image, draw a vertical line from your left shoulder. Draw another line through the center of your upper arm. Measure this angle. Repeat the entire process with your right arm.

Trunk Rotation

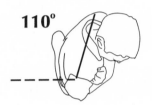

110°

Sit on a chair or stool. Keep your knees pointed straightforward. Turn your shoulders to your right. Do not force the turn. You want to see your unrestricted range. Have someone stand behind you and take a photo or video by pointing the camera down. On the photo or TV image, draw a horizontal line from your right shoulder. Draw another line along the back of your shoulders. Measure the angle between the two lines. Repeat the entire process by turning your shoulders to your left.

How to Evaluate Your Measurements

Divide your range by the minimums shown above (60° Internal Hip Rotation, 90° Arm Flexion, 110° Trunk and Neck Rotation). This will give you the percentage you have. If you have 30° Internal Hip Rotation (the minimum you need for golf is 60°), then you have only 50% of the flexibility you need in your hips for a reliable effortless, effective, efficient swing.

You can play golf with less than full range of motion.

The problem is that it is hard to play well.

If you lack 50% of a needed range, it is no different than trying to play with half the number of clubs, or half the strength you need for golf.

Breathing

You also need at least 15% movement in your stomach, diaphragm and chest when you inhale and exhale. Have someone measure the resting circumference of your belly button, costal arch and nipple line as you lie on your back with your knees up and arms resting by your sides. Inhale all the way and exhale all the way. Measure how many inches each area moves, and divide by the circumference of each area. The result should be a minimum of 15%. For instance, if your chest is 40", it should move a minimum of 6".

If this seems like a lot, we have measured chests that moved 9".

They didn't belong to golfers.

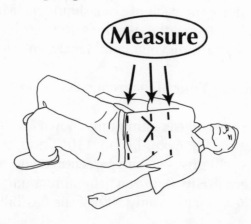

Lying on your back with your knees up, your arms by your side, have someone measure the resting circumference of your abdomen, diaphragm and chest by measuring at your belly button, costal arch (inverted V where your ribs come together in the front) and nipple line (women measured just below the breasts) with a cloth tape measure. When you breathe, be sure to fill both your chest and stomach. In some golfers, the stomach contracts during inhalation. Record that as a negative range (the abdomen should expand when you inhale).

At the top of your backswing, your ribs have to slide past each other for an effortless turn, and your stomach muscles have to stretch. If you do not have at least 15% movement in your stomach and chest, the ribs can't slide and the muscles won't stretch. You will not be able to easily turn your shoulders 120° away from the ball.

You need these minimum ranges so that your body does not interfere with your swing. If you lack any one of these ranges, you have to compensate in your swing because your own stiffness is interfering with the free movement of your body during your swing and putt. The four core ranges and three breathing ranges are only seven of the 44 ranges critical to an efficient golf swing.

If you don't have all of these minimum ranges, you are playing golf with a rusty engine.

Stiffness and Swing Faults

Most swing faults are caused by lack of flexibility in one or more of the 44 ranges you need for an efficient swing. Since golfers are unaware of how much flexibility they have lost, they often attribute their swing faults to lack of concentration. But the cause of most swing faults is physical, not mental.

Stiff Hips

If you do not have 60° of Internal Hip Rotation, you will not be able to freely turn your hips 60° away from the ball at the top of your back swing. You will have to force your turn by tensing up your leg and hip muscles during your backswing. We all know that tension of any kind is the death knell of a reliable swing.

Stiff hips mean that you will start your downswing by sliding your hips to your left, since it is easier to slide stiff hips than it is to turn them.

If your hips are restricted, you will not be able to develop sufficient hip speed for an effortless 280-yard drive. Stiff hips can't turn fast, no more than a rusted engine can operate at a high RPM.

When your hips are stiff and they cannot turn fast, you have to make up for their contribution to clubhead speed by overusing your oblique muscles to power your downswing. Unfortunately, overusing these paper-thin muscles increases your Front Spine Angle during your downswing. As you know from the Alignment chapter, increasing your Front Spine Angle opens up your clubface prior to impact, sending your drives off to the right.

If your hips are really restricted, you will have to reverse pivot in order to get a half-decent turn.

Restricted hips are the main cause of low back pain in golfers (see Chapter Eleven-- Low Back Pain).

Stiff Trunk

If you have less than 110° of Trunk Rotation, you will not be able to produce a good X-factor without increasing your Front Spine Angle at the top of your backswing and, of course, at impact (and you know what increasing your Front Spine Angle will do to your accuracy, don't you?)

If your trunk flexibility is restricted, you will not be able to get separation between Stage Two (your hips) and Stage Three (your shoulders). You can only make up for lack of separation and range with EFFORT.

If you lack flexibility, you have to increase your strength. Lift those weights!

If you lack flexibility, have to practice more. Pound those drives!

If you lack flexibility, you have to hit thousands of balls. Bloody, calloused hands!

The fate of golfers who lack flexibility.

Stiff Neck

If you do not have 110° of Neck Rotation, you will not be able to see the ball with both eyes at the top of your backswing, because the bridge of your nose will cover your right eye.

The golfer on the left has 110⁰ of Neck Rotation, and so can look back over his shoulder at the top of his backswing. The golfer on the right does not, and so cannot see the ball with both eyes, thus losing depth perception. If he wants to hit the ball accurately, he has no choice but to restrict his shoulder turn, which means shorter drives.

Neck stiffness is the single greatest cause of putting problems. If your neck is stiff, as you rotate your shoulders during your backswing, you will pull your eyes off the ball, making contact with the center of your putter very difficult. The biggest improvement we have seen in putters has come from increasing their neck flexibility. One of our pros went from #113 to #1 in Putting Average after we improved his neck rotation.

Stiff Shoulders

If you do not have 90⁰ of Arm Flexion in your left shoulder, you will not be able to achieve a 90⁰ Arm Angle. The stiffer your left shoulder, the more likely you are to start your downswing with your arms and hands. This means you will be casting your club at the Cast Point.

Restricted backswing.

Casting.

Starting from the top.

Not a pretty picture. All due to lack shoulder flexibility.

If you do not have 90⁰ of Arm Flexion in your right shoulder, you will not be able to let the club wrap all the way around your body at the finish of your swing. You need to do this, because at impact your club is traveling at 100+ mph. It takes time and distance to apply the brakes so that your club can come to a complete stop. If you do not have enough flexibility in your right shoulder, you will slow the club down prior to impact in order to slow it down afterwards.

Restricted Breathing

The consequences of restricted breathing are so important that they require a chapter of their own (Chapter 9).

Improving Your Flexibility

Flexibility is so important in golf that it should be spelled flex-ability.

You only have to look at the money list to see the contribution of flexibility to golf.

It is all to the bottom line.

The most flexible golfers on tour are at the top of the list.

The stiffest golfers are at the bottom.

If you do not have 100% of all your ranges, you are not playing with a full set of clubs.

If you do not have these minimum ranges noted above, order our stretching videos (Chapter Fifteen—Training Aids, Resources). If they do not help you achieve your minimum ranges, you need Microfiber Reduction (Chapter Twelve).

The Paradox of Golf

Here is the paradox about golf.

It requires more flexibility than any other sport, but was invented by the stiffest people in the world.

CHAPTER NINE

Breathing

If we are lucky, we get to play golf several times a week.

On the other hand, we breathe 17,280 times a day.

We breathe an average of 12 times a minute, 720 times an hour, 17, 280 times in 24 hours.

17,280 times a day.

120,960 times a week.

483,840 times a month.

5,806,080 times a year.

Anything we do that often, has to be important.

Any problems in that process are going to be repeated 17,280 times every day.

Let's see what some of those problems might be.

Holding your Breath

It's very rare to find a golfer with a minimum of 15% expansion in their stomach, diaphragm and chest. A golfer with a 40" chest should have a minimum of 6" of movement, but we have never found a golfer who does. When we do, he or she will be an exceptional golfer.

We have measured swimmers with 9" of movement in their

chest. When asked if they ever ran out of breath at the end of a race, they looked puzzled by the question.

Golfers with restricted breathing ranges, especially in their chest, tend to hold their breath during their swing. You can always tell, because you can hear a big exhale at the end of the swing.

The problem with holding your breath is that it makes a bad problem worse.

We all know that increasing the amount of shoulder turn in relation to the amount of hip turn at the top of our backswing is going to increase our driving distance. Well-meaning but mistaken teachers recommended restricting the amount of hip turn. Even though computer measurements of professional golfers showed that they turned their hips away from the ball 59-72° at the top of their backswing, teachers started recommending a 45° turn, then a 30° turn, and we actually saw one teacher recommend a 25° hip turn.

The effect, of course, is to rob Stage 2 of all its fuel, and increase the work of Stage 3.

Not very efficient.

It is better to increase the amount of shoulder turn, rather than decrease the amount of hip turn. But you can only do this by increasing the flexibility of your trunk.

When your breathing ranges are tight, your shoulder turn will be restricted.

When you hold your breath, your turn will be restricted even more.

The only way you can hold your breath is to tense up the muscles of your rib cage. This tension will prevent the ribs from sliding past each other, which they have to do with a full turn. When you add tension to an area already stiff, you'll have big problems with your backswing.

We nearly always find that golfers with restricted breathing ranges are breath-holders, and it is impossible for them to change that habit until we improve the flexibility in their breathing ranges.

Does breath-holding create tension and microfibers that restrict the breathing ranges, or do the restricted breathing ranges dispose someone to holding their breath?

It's probably both.

We do know that golfers never get completely comfortable swinging a club until they can do it without holding their breath.

Putting

As you know, an efficient putter uses his stomach muscles, especially the obliques, to make his putting stroke.

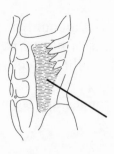

The oblique muscles on the right side rotate the chest to the right during the putt. The arms and shoulders, locked in an unbending triangle, bring the putter along to the top of the backswing. At that point, you relax your stomach muscles and let your putter swing back through the ball for an effortless, efficient, accurate putt.

If your breathing ranges are restricted, however, this will not be easy or effortless. If you are restricted in your abdomen, your left obliques will not easily stretch as you go back to your right, just as your right obliques will not easily stretch as you let your chest rotate to your left during your putting stroke.

Putting requires a delicate touch. You have to bring the putter back just the right amount for the speed and slope of the greens. It is hard to be delicate when your muscles are tense.

Just ask yourself this question: do you want a tense surgeon operating on you? Or, would you rather have one who is relaxed? A tense surgeon can make a little slip of the scalpel and---oops!

The same can happen on the putting green to a golfer with tense stomach muscles. A three-foot putt that shoots past the hole—oops!

The problem is that if you are unaware that your stomach muscles are tight and tense, you will think that your putting problems are purely 'mental'. In 35 years of working with golfers, we have never had one come to us saying 'My breathing ranges are really restricted, and it's ruining my putting'.

In every case, our golfers have been completely unaware of how restricted their breathing had become (even the young ones), and when they found out, didn't believe it could have any impact on their game at all. It was only after we improved their breathing ranges by releasing microfibers in their chests and abdomens (so that they could freely breathe), that they realized how much more relaxed they felt playing golf, and saw how much better they putted.

There are dozens of ways to lose breathing range. Sitting hunched over at a desk eight hours a day. Getting the wind knocked out of you. Falls when young. Chronic or acute mental stress. These are only a few.

The muscles of the trunk are paper-thin. It doesn't take much for them to tense up and start the formation of microfibers. The earlier in life that this happens, the longer the microfibers have to accumulate, and the worse the problem becomes.

This is why so many older golfers stoop over. Their ribs have become glued together, and the glue becomes thicker and thicker with the passage of time, until they are unable to stand up straight.

And they wonder why they can't putt like they used to.

Since each rib forms a joint with its corresponding vertebra, restriction in breathing leads to restriction in the movement of the vertebra. Whereas in a freely moving spine, where each vertebra is able to rotate freely for a smooth putting motion, the spine of someone who has restricted breathing ranges is not a smooth, central axis for the putting stroke. It has kinks: areas that don't move, or don't move easily. It is difficult to have a smooth stroke when the axis you rotate around does not move smoothly.

Heart Disease

You can't play golf when your heart stops beating. Despite all the new diagnostic methods, every year thousands of golfers are surprised by their first heart attack.

For many years, it was thought that cholesterol was the culprit. If it could be controlled, then people would not get heart attacks, but they did. Then other factors were discovered:

high homocysteine, C-reactive protein, and inflammation levels; low HDL, etc.

One factor that has been completely overlooked as a risk factor for heart disease is restricted breathing ranges. We first started to notice that golfers who had had heart attacks all had one inch or less of movement in their rib cage. At first we didn't know if they had restricted breathing because of heart disease, or if restricted breathing contributed to heart disease.

Then we started working with golfers who had the labored breathing that is common to those with heart disease. They also had an expansion of one inch or less.

As we thought about what happens when someone has restricted breathing, it became clear that restricted breathing could be an independent risk factor for heart disease.

When our rib cage is restricted, we breathe shallowly. As a result, we do not blow off carbon dioxide, which is a natural byproduct of our metabolism. The carbon dioxide is heavier than the air we breathe, so it tends to settle in the bottom of our lungs, where most of the gas exchange takes place. Our blood then picks up carbon dioxide instead of oxygen as it passes through the lower third of our lungs. The carbon dioxide, when it dissolves in the bloodstream, makes it slightly acidic. Our blood has to stay in a very narrow pH range, so when it becomes acidic, we pull calcium from our muscles and bones to re-buffer our blood stream. This excess calcium then sticks to cholesterol deposits on our coronary arteries, forming the plaque that eventually narrows, hardens and then blocks the arteries.

One of our golfers came to us with only an inch of expansion in her chest and diaphragm. We told her of our concerns about heart disease, so she went to a well-known clinic for a complete cardiac workup. She passed her stress test, electrocardiogram and blood tests with flying colors. When we asked her if she had a calcium heart scan, she said that the clinic did not want to do one since all her other tests were so good. We urged her to get a scan, which she did. She had so much calcium in her coronary arteries that she was in the 90th percentile for heart attack risk.

The clinic was shocked at the results. She immediately went on an aggressive program of supplementation, exercise, and diet. While she has not reduced her calcium scores, she has increased her protective HDL, reduced her body fat, and increased her overall fitness. She is grateful that she did not find out that she had heart disease the way most people do—by having a heart attack.

Osteoporosis

We mentioned that when breathing is shallow, carbon dioxide builds up in the lower third of the lungs and dissolves in the bloodstream, making it acidic. Calcium is withdrawn from the muscles and bones to rebuffer the bloodstream.

When calcium is pulled from the muscles, the muscles tense up, because calcium is a muscle relaxant. This exacerbates our shallow breathing because our breathing muscles tense up even more.

But the real concern, apart from heart disease, is osteoporosis. Shallow breathing is also a risk factor for this all too common disease.

Years ago we worked with a client whose osteoporosis was so severe that she had fractured three vertebrae just bending over to work in her garden. She was in such severe pain that her husband had to buy a van and install a bed in the back so that they could travel, as going over the slightest bump or hole in the road would jar her spine when she was sitting up and cause intense pain.

We were apprehensive about working with someone who was in such bad straights, but she said she had tried everything to reduce her pain, and nothing had helped. We found her breathing range was only 3/4''' in her chest, and 1/4" in her diaphragm. We gently released microfibers in those areas and her breathing immediately improved. She came to see us several times a week for three months, and by the end of her program with us, she was able to ride sitting up in the front seat and was free of pain. She returned to her physician for her scheduled bone scan and was pleased to see that her bone density had increased by 10%, her first improvement after years of progressively thinning bones.

Course Management

In addition to interfering with the efficient use of our clubs and putter, restricted breathing also affects our course management.

The brain runs on just oxygen and sugar (glucose). You are probably aware of how fuzzy your thinking becomes if you haven't eaten for many hours, and how your thinking is restored once you get something to eat.

The same applies to breathing.

Shallow breathing brought on by restriction in the chest, diaphragm or abdomen increases the amount of carbon dioxide in our bloodstream and reduces the amount of oxygen that gets to our tissues.

Our brain weighs only 5% of our body mass, but consumes 20% of the oxygen we breathe, which means our brain consumes four times more oxygen than any other part of our body.

The part of our body that pays the highest price for shallow breathing is our brain.

If your breathing is restricted, it has probably been getting progressively tighter and tighter every year for many years. The loss of oxygen to your brain is very likely not noticeable. Unlike restriction in calories, where you can see yourself losing weight and your clothes becoming looser, you cannot tell that your brain is getting less oxygen.

First of all, you would need awareness of lack of oxygen, and you rely on your brain for awareness. If your brain is on an oxygen-restricted diet because of stiffness in your breathing ranges, you brain will not be functioning at its maximum, and part and parcel of that is less acute awareness.

In nursing homes, the treatment of choice for dementia is administration of pure oxygen.

It is not really feasible to carry oxygen with you on the course (but we would not be surprised to see people try it!), and you don't really need supplemental oxygen if you improve your breathing ranges.

Many of our clients have reported an increased sense of awareness after we improved their breathing ranges. Many of them have noticeably improved facial color and a more youthful appearance, as the calcium leaves their bloodstream and returns to relax the muscles of their face. Those who depend on invention and creativity in their business report that both increase as their breathing ranges improve. All of them report that they feel more confident, and make better decisions in club choice and course management.

Years ago, two psychologists, who were also avid golfers, completed our program. Being psychologists, there were acutely aware of the psychological changes that occurred. They asked to test our clients before and after their program to see if everyone experienced the same changes.

In one year, all of our clients completed the Adjective Check List (a list of 200 adjectives that you choose from to describe yourself) before starting their program with us. They filled out the Adjective Check List a second time to describe their ideal self. Once they completed our program, they filled out the two forms a second time. The psychologists were surprised to see that everyone's ideal self remained stable, but their self-description, in many cases, now matched their ideal. They said that they had never seen such a dramatic change reported in any of the psychology literature.

Low Back Pain

As you will see in the chapter on Low Back Pain, it is not caused by problems in the low back, even if they do exist. An MRI study at a major hospital found that 1170 of 1500 patients completely free of back pain had ruptured or bulging discs in their lower back.

We have found, and others have confirmed, that lower back pain is caused by restrictions in the hips and mid-back. Because the areas above and below the lower back are restricted, all the stress of movement is concentrated in the lower back, and it responds with spasm and pain.

The major cause of mid-back tightness is restriction in breathing, especially around the diaphragm. The posterior inferior serratus muscles go from the spine to the lower ribs. They are the coughing muscles. You can see them work if you stand behind someone with their shirt off and ask them to cough.

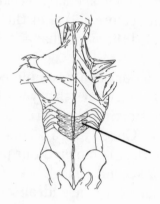

The posterior inferior serratus are small muscles that go from the spine to the lower ribs. If they are tied up with microfibers, your lower ribs will not be able to move, and your breathing and mid-back will be restricted.

If you have had colds, allergies, bronchitis, or pneumonia, your coughing muscles had to work overtime and microfibers formed around them. If you fell on your back, got punched on the playground, or fell on a ball and got the wind knocked out of you, these muscles spasmed, and more microfibers formed. As these muscles became tighter, and more microfibers formed in your mid-back, your breathing became more and more restricted.

You can test for restriction in this area in two ways. The first is to measure your expansion around your diaphragm.

The second is to lie prone on the floor, with your arms by your side. Raise your nose as far off the floor as you can. If you do not have restrictions in your mid-back, you will be able to raise your nose a minimum of 24" off the floor.

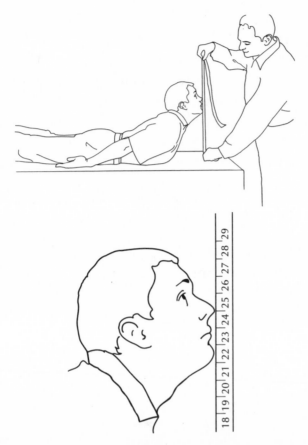

Lie on your stomach on a firm bed or on the floor. Let your arms lie relaxed beside you. Using only your back muscles, lift up your nose as far off the resting surface as you can. Have someone measure the distance. The minimum you need for golf is 24".

Improving Your Breathing Ranges

If you didn't pass the breathing or back-extension measuring tests, get our Breathing DVD (Chapter 15) and start stretching your breathing ranges. If that does not help, you have microfibers in your trunk, and need Microfiber Reduction (Chapter 12).

CHAPTER TEN

The Yips

When you believe the body is composed of muscles, bones and nerves, you look for the cause of the yips in one of these three systems. Since it is unlikely that someone's hands would shake while holding a putter because of their bones, this leaves the muscles and nerves as prime suspects.

The yip police have spent decades investigating and (falsely) accusing the muscles and nerves.

When you realize that everything in the body is encased in a thin membrane of connective tissue, you begin to wonder: could this pervasive connective tissue contribute to creating the yips?

Here is a model of the muscles and connective tissue.

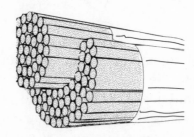

This model shows that a thin membrane of connective tissue called fascia surrounds each and every muscle. Inside of our body, the muscles never touch each other. Only their surrounding membranes actually touch. These membranes are normally smooth, and have a lubricating fluid between them. The purpose of these membranes is to allow the muscles to slide past each other, which they have to do in order to stretch or contract.

Here is a cross-section of the neck, with everything removed but the connective tissue membranes.

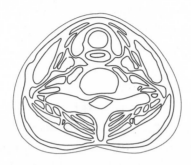

This cross-section of the neck shows how pervasive the connective tissue is in our body. Everything has been removed but the connective tissue. Every muscle, bone, nerve, blood vessel and internal organ has its own layer of connective tissue.

Here is a cross-section of the forearm, with everything removed but the connective tissue membranes.

There is a thick layer of connective tissue just below the skin that surrounds all the muscles. Underneath this thick layer, each muscle has it own membrane. The role of the connective tissue is to facilitate movement. It serves the same purpose as

cartilage (another form of connective tissue) does
in the joints.

Our suspicions about the role of the connective tissue in the
yips were first aroused when we started looking at how professional golfers solved the centrifugal force problem. How
did historically great golfers make contact with the center of
the clubface when the club was being pulled from their hands
with 100 lbs. of force and traveling at 110+ mph?

The usual method is to change the spine angle to compensate
for the six or seven inches that the arm and club shaft length-
en from address to impact. To adjust for this added length,
most golfers stand up during their downswing. This, of course,
means years of practice so that they can stand up exactly the
right amount to compensate for the 100 lbs. of pull and still
make contact with an area the size of a postage stamp in the
center of the clubface.

We were startled to see that some well-known pros did not
change their spine angle between address and impact.

How did they do this and still maintain contact with the center of the clubface?

The answer was in their Wrist Angle—the angle between their
forearm and club shaft.

The pros who were maintaining their Spine Angle were also
maintaining their Wrist Angle.

Instead of letting their wrists extend, they were gripping their
clubs with so much pressure that they were able to resist 100
lbs. of pull with their small forearm muscles.

This is what they looked like.

Here is a golfer at address with a 20° Wrist Angle, or a 20° difference between his arm and his club-shaft.

This is the same golfer at impact. He has been able to achieve good ball contact because he has maintained his Wrist Angle. There has been no increase in the distance between his shoulders and club-head.

We realized why these golfers were so good. They returned their clubshaft at impact to exactly the same position it had at address. Because of this, they were all excellent ball strikers.

We were amazed that they were able to grip the club hard

enough to resist 100 lbs. of pull!

But further research raised an ominous co-incidence.

All of these well-known pros developed the yips later in their career.

In other words, yippers were grippers.

To appreciate the amount of force you have to exert with your hands in order to maintain your Wrist Angle at impact, try this experiment with a friend. Stand at address with your driver, with your hands relaxed in their conventional address position. Keeping your Wrist Angle constant, stand up straight so that your club shaft is horizontal. Be sure you maintain your original Wrist Angle. Have a friend hold on to the club head and lean away from you (make sure you are doing this in a safe environment, just in case the clubhead comes off the clubshaft). Try to resist any straightening of your arms and club shaft. In a few moments, you will feel tremendous strain in the muscles of your forearms. Some even find their forearms shaking with the effort.

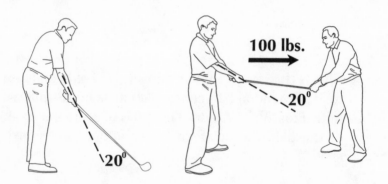

Stand at your normal hands-dropped address position. Without changing your arm position or Wrist Angle, stand up straight. Have someone pull the club away from you by holding on and leaning back (make sure you are both standing in a safe area, in case of a fall). Grip your club as hard as you can to prevent your arms and the club from straightening.

This 100 lbs. of pull takes place in a fraction of a second during an actual swing. It happens so fast that a golfer would be unaware of the contraction he needs to exert with his muscles to prevent any change in his wrist angle. A serious golfer would repeat this contraction of his forearm muscles hundreds of times a day, for weeks, months and years on end.

In order to maintain enough grip pressure on the club to prevent any extension, you have to exert phenomenal amount of tension with the muscles of your forearms. As you will see in the chapter on Microfiber Reduction (Chapter 12), tension creates microfibers in the connective tissue between the muscles. These microfibers bind the muscles together. They also accumulate over time, making the forearms stiffer and stiffer as years go by.

We have also found that, in addition to binding the muscles together, microfibers, through a process we do not understand, also bind tension into place. When we release microfibers, we can feel the muscles relax. Our clients can often feel the same relaxation. They will often proclaim surprise at how soft their muscles feel. Before we released their microfibers, the muscles in that area felt hard to the touch. 'Knots in the muscles' is the usual description. In some areas the knots were painful. Once the microfibers around those 'knots' were released, the muscles relaxed and the painful knots disappeared.

We find many microfibers and very hard muscles are in the forearms of golfers who have or had problems with habitually over-gripping their clubs. The forearm muscles are very small. They were not designed to maintain the wrist angle during a 100 lb. pull at 100+ mph. As we release the microfibers in the forearms, the muscles soften and relax, and these golfers find that they can relax their grip pressure while putting.

This is what a yip-free golfer looks like at address and impact. Notice that this golfer has 'gone ballistic'. He has let his wrists extend. Instead of fighting centrifugal force, he has elected to go with it.

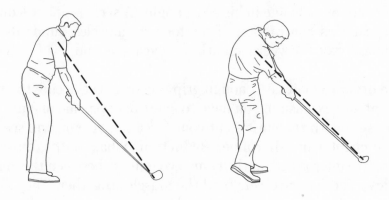

> This is the address and impact position of a yip-free golfer. He allows his arms and club to extend with the centrifugal force pulling the club away from him. He has elected to go with the force instead of fighting it.

While this strategy saves our 'ballistic' golfer from the yips, it creates another problem, which is making good ball contact. A golfer using this strategy has to decrease his Spine Angle exactly the right amount to make up for the 6-7" of extension caused by giving in to centrifugal force. If he stands up too much, he will hit the ball thin. If he stands up too little, he will hit it fat.

Holding your Wrist Angle in order to improve your ball contact seems like a smart move. Some of the best golfers in history went down this path. But they ended up with the yips.

It was a heavy price to pay. If they knew that they would get the yips from maintaining their Wrist Angle, they might have re-thought their decision. The yips seemed to them to be the cruel hand of fate, but were, in fact, the result of a decision they all made, conscious or otherwise. They often suffered at the apex of their game. It was a terrible finish to otherwise brilliant careers.

The yips can be avoided and good ball contact can be maintained just by placing your hands on the swing plane at address. Not grounding the club at address is an easy way to achieve this extension. In this way, you can swing freely, knowing that your arms and clubshaft will not extend very much because they are already extended.

We recommend you do this with all your clubs, not just your driver. The simple act of placing your hands on your swing plane will increase the accuracy of all your clubs.

Lately, we have seen that some of the pros are 'sneaking' up on the swing plane. They are holding their hands higher at address. Not on the swing plane, but higher than before. As a result, they are playing better than ever. We don't know if they are doing this themselves, or at the behest of their teacher, but the results speak for themselves.

So move your hands all the way to the swing plane at address. It looks 'different', but it makes so much sense. Better ball contact. More accuracy. Less chance of developing the yips.

With your arms on the swing plane at address, you can make good ball contact and sleep easy, knowing that you will not develop the yips.

If you already have the yips, then consider Microfiber Reduction (Chapter 12) to get rid of the microfibers in your forearms (and everywhere else you have them).

Low Back Pain

Low back pain has become rampant in golf. A recent study found that fully 1/3rd of professional golfers at a single tournament had suffered low back pain of more than two weeks duration during the prior year that affected their play. The rise in low back pain in golf coincides with the introduction of the 'compact' swing, lifting weights and running. In other words, the 'modern' approach to golf has spawned a new industry: repairing the lower back.

As we have stated before, the compact swing increases the accelerative, shearing forces on the whole body, thereby increasing the strain on the ligaments, tendons, muscles and joints. Couple this with the stiffness produced by lifting weights and running and you have a recipe for disaster.

Conventional approaches to low back pain focus on the low back itself. Surgery, injections, strengthening the abdominals, adjustments, etc. all try to fix something 'wrong' with the low back area. After all, the theory goes, if the pain is in the lower back, the cause of the pain must be there as well.

This type of thinking, which we call 'proxitis', looks for the cause of a problem at or near the site of the problem. Proxitis is a disease that is rampant in medicine and sports, which is why so much attention is paid to the grip in golf, since the hands are the part of the body nearest the club. The wisdom of 'proxitis' seems to have been confirmed by the use of the MRI, which is able to clearly image ruptured (herniated) or bulging discs at or near the site of the pain in the lower back.

An interesting study was done several years ago at a major hospital. MRI's were taken of 1500 individuals who had abso-

The Efficient Golfer   103

lutely no history of lower back pain. 1170 of these individuals had ruptured or herniated discs. If so many pain-free individuals have ruptured or bulging discs, it seems doubtful that they are the cause of low back pain, does it not?

We have worked with many golfers and tennis players who suffered from chronic lower back pain. We have found that lower back pain is not caused by herniated discs, but by restricted movement in the hips and middle back. By releasing microfibers that surround the muscles in the hips and middle back, we have been able to return golfers to the course and tennis players to the court either pain-free or with so much less discomfort that they are able to enjoy their favorite game once again. In the thirty-five years we have been working with athletes with low back pain, we have never actually worked on the lower back. We have found, over and over again, that the lower back is the only part of the body that has normal movement. It is the restrictions above and below the lower back that focus strain on this area. As a result of this stress and strain, the area becomes inflamed, the small muscles go into spasm, and you have pain.

Our theory about the origin of low back pain in golf is that the cause is purely mechanical. When a golfer swings the club through the ball, the head of the club is traveling 100+ mph and pulling away from the golfer with 100 lbs. of force. This is the same amount of force you would experience in lifting a 100 lb. bag of cement. The momentum of the club and upper body causes the upper body to continue to rotate after impact. If a golfer has restrictions in his hips from microfibers (often created by jogging, lifting weights, or prior falls and injuries) the hips will suddenly stop turning. When the hips stop turning, while the upper body continues to turn, the stress on the lower back is tremendous. Muscles are strained, inflammation sets in, more muscles tense up, and you have a vicious cycle of contraction and pain.

As we said above, we have never touched a painful lower back. For most golfers, it is the only part of the body that works correctly. Increasing the flexibility of the lower back will only further increase the imbalances already in the body.

We concentrate our work on the hips, increasing their range so that the hips can continue to turn after impact. As the hips become more flexible, the strain on the lower back is reduced, and the pain is either eliminated or reduced.

At address, most golfers turn out their left foot 30^0. At the finish of their swing, their hips have rotated 90^0 or more to the left. In order to finish the golf swing with your hips square to the target, without the hips stopping prematurely, and thus straining the lower back, you need a minimum of 60^0 of internal hip rotation on the left hip

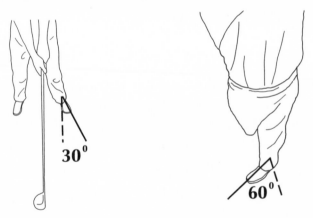

You also need 60^0 of internal hip rotation on the right hip in order to turn your hips 60^0 away from the ball at the top of your backswing.

You can measure your internal hip rotation by lying on your stomach with your legs together. Bend both knees 90^0 so that your feet point toward the ceiling. Keeping your knees together, move your feet away from each other. Have someone take a picture or video of your lower legs. Draw vertical lines through your knees and lines through the center of your lower legs. Measure the angle between the leg lines and the vertical. The angle should be a minimum of 60⁰. If it is less, and you have lower back pain, you have taken the first step to recovery: you have identified the cause of your pain.

The next step is to see if you have restrictions in your middle back. Lying on your stomach with your arms by your sides,

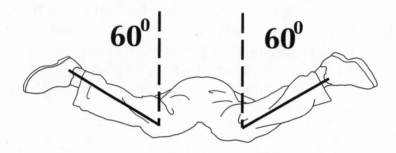

lift your nose off the floor as high as you can. Have someone measure the distance from your nose to the floor. It should be a minimum of 24 inches. If not, you have discovered another cause of your lower back pain.

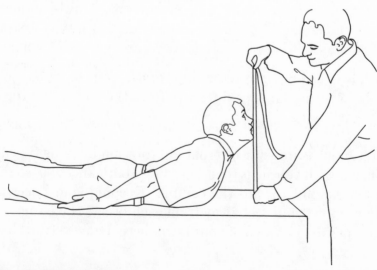

You'll first want to see if stretching can improve your measurements. We have a stretch for internal hip rotation in our DVD *Are You Flexible Enough for Golf?* We also have a stretch to increase back extension in our DVD *Breathing*.

If stretching does not help you achieve full range of motion in your hips and middle back, the problem is microfibers that have formed in these areas. Getting the wind knocked out of you causes most of the microfibers in the middle back. This can be due to falls, getting punched or kicked in the stomach, getting tackled in football or soccer, or getting hit in the stomach by a football, basketball or soccer ball. Another common cause is chronic coughing. The coughing muscles (posterior inferior serratus) are right in the middle of the back. You can see them contract if you watch someone from the back coughing. Chronic coughing from allergies, bronchitis, pneumonia or colds causes these muscles to tense up and form microfibers. The area gets progressively stiffer as you get older due to the accumulation of microfibers.

Constriction in the hips is usually caused by falls on our rear end when we are young: falls on the playground, ball field, tennis or basketball court; falls off bikes, ladders, stairs, trees, rooftops, horses, etc. Running creates microfibers in the hips; as do squats, leg presses and plyometrics.

We first published our findings on low back pain in the August 1993 issue of **Golf** magazine. Our findings were confirmed 11 years later in an article published in the **American Journal of Sports Medicine** in April of 2004. The study, by Vad, et al, reported the findings of a survey of golfers playing in the 2001 Buick Classic in New York. One-third of the golfers in this tournament had suffered low back pain during the prior year for two weeks or more that affected their quality of play. The player's average age was only 31 years of age. The players with pain had significantly less internal hip rotation in their lead hip, and significantly less back extension.

While the authors of the study lay the blame for decreased flexibility in the hips and middle back on the golf swing, we do not find that this is the case. When we release microfibers in these areas, golfers remember stress that pre-dated their golf careers, such as falls, impacts, or stress that occurred when they were young.

If the golf swing itself was the cause of loss of flexibility, then the golfers who were pain free should have had the same loss of flexibility as the golfers with pain. Blaming loss of flexibility on the golf swing is just another example of 'proxitis': if golfers have loss of flexibility (and the lower back pain that comes with it), it must be due to the golf swing.

We find that much of the increase in hip tightness has nothing to do with golf. It can be traced to falls, running and weight lifting. As we state in our chapter on Microfiber Reduction (Chapter 12), even an elite distance runner lands with about 1,000 lbs. of force on each leg when they run. With 1,000 strides per mile, on a five-mile run, a runner has to endure

5,100,000 lbs. of force pounding down on their legs. This pounding tears the small muscle fibers in the hips and legs, creating microfibers in the connective tissue surrounding these muscles. Once the muscle fibers have healed, the microfibers not only do not go away, they tend to accumulate over time, making runners stiffer as they get older. When we work with golfers who have been running for some time to keep in shape, they often recall the soreness they felt while running.

Leg presses, dead lifts, squats, and bent over rows all create microfibers in the hips and back. We know this to be true, because our clients recall these stresses as we release microfibers in their legs, hips and middle backs.

As we have said before, other causes of stiffness in the hips are the common injuries we have all suffered at one time or another: sliding into base while playing baseball; stopping and starting on the tennis court; falling on your rear end; injuring your tail bone; falling off bicycles or horses, out of trees, off ladders, down stairs; tripping over stones, logs, and other obstacles while hiking; getting tackled during football or soccer; and having your feet swept out from under you in basketball.

To see examples of how we have successfully eliminated low back pain in our golfers, please look through Case Histories (Chapter 13).

One client you won't see there is a golfer who came to us with lower back pain so severe he was unable to play for the prior two years. As with all the golfers we have worked with who suffered low back pain, he lacked flexibility in his hips and middle back. As we released microfibers in these areas, he was able to swing his clubs pain-free. He mentioned he was going to Florida after his last session with us. We cautioned him not to play too much golf, as his muscles would be weak from lack of use for the past two years, and from being immobilized in the internal 'cast' created by the microfibers around them.

Like most golfers we have worked with, he did not listen to our plea for moderation. He went to Florida and played two rounds a day for four days straight without any pain at all.

CHAPTER TWELVE

Microfiber Reduction

There has been tremendous progress in the last decade in golf equipment because scientists have re-engineered clubs and balls.

Now we can re-engineer the golfer's body—the most important piece of equipment on the course. We do this by releasing microfibers that are binding the body together with an invisible cast. Taking off that cast (which every golfer has to some extent or another), allows the golfer to play the game efficiently, moving without impediment.

Microfibers are a mild type of scar tissue that form between the muscles as a result of injury, illness, overuse or stress.

Microfibers form through a process we call **STMR** (pronounced 'stammer')

Stress
Tension
Microfibers
Restriction

The most common reaction to stress of any kind is that we tense our muscles. We tense our muscles in our shoulders when we are under the pressure of a deadline. We tense the muscles in our chest when we have a cold. We tense the muscles in our hips when the small, individual muscle fibers are torn by running or lifting weights, or when we fall on our rear end on the playground.

Most of the time, we are not aware that we are tensing our muscles.

When we tense our muscles, the connective tissue, which is not very bright, believes we have broken a bone. It immediately starts to develop microfibers, a very mild form of scar tissue, between the layers of connective tissue that surround all the muscles in the area. These microfibers bind adjacent layers of connective tissue together to prevent sliding, which is necessary for the muscles to stretch. By preventing movement in the area, they function as an internal cast. Once they have formed, however, the microfibers not only do not go away, they tend to accumulate over time, making golfers (and everyone else) stiffer as they get older.

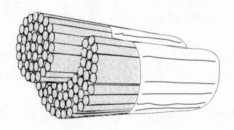

This is a model of the muscles and connective tissue. A thin membrane of connective tissue surrounds each muscle in our body. Normally, this connective tissue is smooth to facilitate the muscles sliding past each other, which they have to do in order to stretch or contract. But when the muscles tense up (due to injury, illness, overuse, or stress), microfibers form in between the connective tissue layers surrounding the muscles to prevent this sliding movement. This helps to immobilize the area so that it can heal. Once the stress is gone, however, the microfibers not only do not go away, they tend to accumulate over time, making people stiffer as they get older.

Just as with an external cast, stretching cannot release microfibers. It would not make sense to create a cast that could be stretched out. If you happened to stretch before two broken bones were completely knitted together, and the microfibers were released, the ends of the two bones would come apart, and that leg, arm or rib would never heal.

The problem is that we don't see this internal cast. We are unaware of our connective tissue and the whole process of microfibrosis. We go out to play golf in our invisible cast, and wonder why we don't succeed.

Stress

The stresses that lead to the formation of microfibers (and eventual loss of flexibility) are as varied as life itself. Here is a list. Check off how many of these stresses have occurred in your lifetime. The earlier in your life, the greater the loss of flexibility, as microfibers accumulate over time. Remember, none of these have to be serious enough to go to a doctor or hospital. You don't need a cut or bruise. It does not have to be painful. Just an impact will do.

Injuries

Fall off bike
Fall off skateboard
Fall skiing
Fall water-skiing
Fall on ice
Fall off ladder
Fall out of tree
Fall off roof
Fall down stairs
Fall on playground
Fall on wet floor
Fall while hiking
Fall on tennis court
Fall on basketball court
Fall on running track
Fall on job
Collisions in football
Collisions in baseball
Collisions in hockey
Collisions in basketball
Collisions in soccer
Collisions in field hockey
Collisions in lacrosse
Collisions in rugby
Collisions in water polo
Sliding into base
Hit by baseball
Hit by bat
Hit in stomach by football
Hit in stomach by basketball
Hit in stomach by soccer ball

Tackled in soccer
Elbowed in soccer
Belly flop in pool
Back flop in pool
Drowning
Punched
Kicked
Bitten
Choked
Hit by car
Hit by bicyclist
Hit by motorcyclist
Auto accident
Bicycle accident
Motorcycle accident
Boating accident
Industrial accident
Bruise
Broken bone
Laceration
Muscle tear
Muscle pull
Sprained back
Twisted ankle
Sprained wrist
Sprained elbow
Twisted neck
Whiplash
Concussion
Head injury

Overuse

Throwing a baseball
Passing a football
Serving a tennis ball
Ice-skating
Running
Stadium stairs
Running on a tennis court
Push-ups
Pull-ups
Sit-ups
'Core' work
Lifting weights
Carrying a backpack
Carrying a briefcase
Carrying a golf bag
Lifting heavy objects
Hitting hundreds of range balls

Illness

Colds
Bronchitis
Allergies
Pneumonia
Hepatitis
Ear infections
Polio

Medical

Surgery
Forceps during childbirth
Tonsillectomy
Appendectomy
Coronary bypass
Epidural injection

Protracted labor
Cast
Crutches
Hospitalization
Orthotics

Mental Stress

Job stress
Marital stress
Economic stress
School stress
Fear
Pain
Anger
Childhood abuse
Abusive teachers
Abusive bosses
Abusive spouse
Loss of parent
Loss of child
Loss of sibling
Loss of grandparent
Loss of pet
Chronic frustration

Miscellaneous

Smoking
Sitting at a desk for long periods of time
Pulling shoulders back to stand up 'straight'
Leg length differences
Wearing high heels

We know these stresses produce microfibers, because our clients have recalled them when we have released microfibers in the affected areas. If we are releasing microfibers around the hips, clients may recall a fall on their rear end. If we release microfibers from the shoulder area, they may recall pitching fastballs with a sore arm when they were in Little League. When we release microfibers in their neck, they may remember a mild whiplash in a car accident, falling while skiing or chronic ear infections when they were young. When we release microfibers that are constricting their breathing, they may recall an old habit of smoking, or bronchitis they had when they were a kid. But if you were to ask them before we worked with them if any of these events could be affecting their golf swing, they would vigorously deny it, if they remembered the events at all.

Just as microfibers do not go away after a stressful incident, the stress itself can also endure over time. Often just remembering the stress at the time the microfibers are released is enough to get rid of it. If not, we have developed Stress Reduction, a program that can target the stress directly. It is particularly effective with stresses that persist, either because they were chronic, or the stress was overwhelming at the time.

Tension

As we said above, the most common response to any kind of stress is muscle tension. We tense our muscles. But what purpose does tension serve?

When we break a bone, the purpose of the resulting tension is to force the two ends to stay in contact with each other so that they can knit back together again.

But what purpose is served by tensing our muscles after a fall, or when we overuse them?

The purpose of tension is local analgesia, or pain reduction.

Pain Reduction

Imagine if you are in a fight with someone. They stab you with a spear. The wound has not caused much damage, but it has caused quite a bit of pain. If this pain disabled you, you might lose the fight. If, on the other hand, you could quickly anesthetize the area, you could continue to fight.

Tension is your local anesthesia.

Tension numbs an area. We know this is true, because we find that people are often unaware of an area when it is very tense. We once worked with a client with a very tense lower back. We asked him to put his hand behind his back and touch the base of his spine. He touched an area well above the base, right where the tension started to diminish.

We have also found that people who are very tense have poor proprioception. They cannot feel what is going on in their body. People who have very little tension, on the other hand, usually have excellent proprioception. They can feel everything.

When we work with golfers who are very stiff, we notice that they often deny 'feeling' stiff. As we work with them, releasing microfibers to improve their flexibility, their muscles started to relax. Surprisingly, many of them then complain about 'feeling' stiff. It is only by showing them photos and measurements of their ranges that we are able to convince them that they are more flexible, even though they 'feel' stiffer. For many years, we were puzzled by this reaction, and unable to explain it.

On the other hand, if we have a client who is very flexible

except for one area of their body, they complain about feeling stiff, and exclaim how much better they feel after we release a small number of microfibers in the one area that was tight. Why are these people so much better at feeling what is going on in their bodies than those who are tense and stiff?

After years of reflection, it finally dawned on us the protective advantage of tension. It numbs the area. Unfortunately, if someone is tense all over, they are also numb all over.

The Brain

Analgesia also occurs in the brain. Whenever you get injured, or there is even the threat of injury, your brain immediately releases endorphins, an endogenous form of a painkiller 400 times stronger than morphine. These endorphins are not released into your bloodstream where they have to travel over time to your brain. They go directly into your brain cells. The endorphins act as a painkiller and a sedative, so that you don't go into shock. Here are two examples of the power of endorphins:

One of our clients was a skilled rider. One day, while riding at full speed, his horse stepped in a hole and came to a sudden stop. He shot forward out of his saddle, striking the ground with his chest. He tore up about ten feet of the ground he landed on. His wife, who was watching nearby, thought that he was either dead or paralyzed. She was shocked to see him get up, jump back on his horse, and continue to ride. About 2 am the next morning, he woke with terrible pains in his chest, made worse with every breath he took. He went to the doctor that day and an X-ray showed three broken ribs! Needless to say, a decade later, we released many microfibers in that area of his chest.

But you don't have to break a bone to release endorphins. Sometimes just the threat of an injury is enough to trigger tension and an endorphin release (and create microfibers):

A client was driving home at night on a dark, icy road. Turning a bend in the road, she noticed a truck on the meridian ahead. She didn't pay much attention to it, until she was right up on it. Then she notice that long iron girders were sticking out of the rear of the trunk, into her lane. She hit the brakes, but the car skidded forward on the ice. At the last minute, she leaned over to her right and pulled her daughter's head down. The girders sheared off the top of their car. Thankfully, neither of them was injured. She felt surprisingly well because of the endorphins that her brain had released as her car skidded on the ice. She didn't even remember the accident when we asked her to write down all her accidents on her history sheet. But twenty years later she had a right-bending scoliosis in her spine that no one could explain. As we released the microfibers along the right side of her spine, her legs started shaking and she recalled the accident. She felt cold and briefly re-experienced the fear of that incident twenty years ago. After her legs stopped shaking, she stood up. Her spine was perfectly straight. She felt more relaxed all over.

Again, you don't have to experience this much trauma to tense up. We worked with a very talented basketball player who was able to recall every impact he received on court as we released microfibers in his legs, arms and back. He also recalled diving on the court for loose balls as we released microfibers in the front of his rib cage.

Reversing STMR

Once we release the microfibers from between the muscles, we notice that often the muscles will relax. When this happens, people often recall the stress that initiated the formation of microfibers in that area.

In effect, we are reversing the stammer (STMR) process. We

find the areas that are restricted by measuring the ranges needed for an activity. Then we release the microfiber in that area. As we release the microfibers, the muscles often relax, tension is reduced, and our client recalls the stress.

Sometimes people do not relax and do not recall the original stress. In these cases, new microfibers form because of the residual tension. But once the tension and microfibers are released, that area will stay loose, unless it is injured, overuse, or tensed up again.

For those clients who don't readily relax, we have developed Tension Reduction exercises. With Tension Reduction we can pinpoint specific muscle groups for relaxation. This is better than procedures for overall relaxation (meditation, hypnosis, drugs) because everyone has a pattern of tension. Some muscles are more relaxed than others. Some remain tense all the time. Some tense and relax, depending on circumstances. By selectively reducing tension in specific muscles, we can change the pattern of tension.

If two muscles can perform the same task, the muscle that is tighter will always contract first. At the top of your backswing, whichever muscles are tightest in your body at the time will contract first during your downswing. If you cannot target specific muscles for relaxation, you cannot change this pattern. It is one of the things that makes it so hard for golfers to change their swing. The other, of course, is microfibers. Even if you were able to relax muscles that were bound together with microfibers, they still would not be able to stretch at the top of your backswing.

Microfibers and Tension

We have found that microfibers not only bind muscles together, they also bind tension into place. A good example is the lady above who was in the car accident. Her muscles along the right side of her spine were tighter to the touch than the muscles along the left side of her spine. When we released the microfibers along the right side of her spine, those same muscles spontaneously relaxed, and were just as relaxed as the muscles on the left.

Muscles and microfibers interact in two ways. Tension in the muscles triggers the formation of microfibers, which in turn bind the muscles together and bind the tension in place.

Most people mistakenly assume that once a stress has passed, there are no after-effects. The tension we experienced at the moment (if we even remember it after our brain has been bathed with endorphins) passes with time – or so we believe. We are not aware of the formation of microfibers, so we assume we are 'alright' after sufficient time has passed.

Stiffness and Age

When we find ourselves getting stiffer, it is a big mystery to us. Where does this stiffness come from? Why does stretching not help? Are our joints getting stiff? Whatever it is, it must be inevitable, as everyone gets stiffer as they get older.

Just one more indignity to suffer with age.

With Microfiber Reduction, the stiffness of old age can be reversed. If you are still young, but are stiff, then you can be more flexible.

Microfiber Reduction can level the playing field, so that you have the same freedom of movement as your competitors.

It can do more.

You can have more flexibility than your competitors. You can make the playing field uneven in your favor.

Microfibers

A physician who performed autopsies on the legs of marathoners and noted a proliferation of connective tissue everywhere first coined the terms 'microfibers'. He named this proliferation 'microfibrosis'. He did not understand why it was happening.

How Microfibers Form

We now know that it was a reaction to the tearing of muscle fibers caused by marathoners bouncing up and down as they run. With just a three-inch bounce, a marathoner lands with six times his body weight with each stride he takes. A marathoner weighing 170 lbs. lands with 1,020 lbs. of force on each leg. Taking an average of 1,000 strides a mile for 26.2 miles, or 26,200 strides, marathoners' legs absorb 26,724,000 lbs. (13,362 tons) of force in a single marathon.

When muscle fibers tear, enzymes are released into the blood stream. Researchers have found these enzymes in the blood of marathoners as much as six weeks after completing a marathon.

We also know that in addition to scar tissue forming within the muscles during the repair process, microfibers, a very mild form of scar tissue, also form in between the connective membranes (fascia) surrounding the muscles. By binding together the adjacent connective tissue membranes, the microfibers prevent sliding motion between muscles, which has to take place for the muscles to stretch. Microfibers are nature's internal cast. They form to immobilize the area so that it can heal. Unfortunately, once the muscles have finally repaired from all the damage they suffered from running a marathon (or any other running), the microfibers not only do not go away, they tend to accumulate over time, making runners stiffer as they get older. Little wonder that we have found that marathoners are the stiffest of all athletes.

This process of microfibrosis takes place anytime you have an overuse injury to the muscles. It does not have to be a marathon run. We often find microfibers in between the small muscles of the left shoulder blade in golfers. We find them there because these golfers are powering their downswing with their small shoulder muscles, instead of using their larger and more powerful leg and hip muscles.

We have also learned that muscle fibers do not need to tear in order for microfibers to form. Microfibers can form just from tension alone. If you break a bone, the surrounding muscles will tense up in an effort to keep the ends of the bones together so that they can heal. If you have a tough day at the office (or on the golf course) and you tense up your shoulder muscles, microfibers will also form.

The connective tissue is not very bright. It cannot tell the difference between a broken bone and a bad day.

Microfibers can form from activities as innocuous as chronically holding your breath, or leaning over a desk for eight hours a day, or over-gripping your club.

Microfibers and Genetics

The propensity to form microfibers is genetic. Some people form them more readily than others. Adhesions, another form of scar tissue, often form after abdominal surgery. For some people, they form so readily that additional surgery is required to remove them. For others, the formation of adhesions is minimal. The same is true with microfibers.

We saw this difference in microfiber formation when we worked with a rowing team made up of rugby players. Most of the rowers on this team were very stiff from years of banging into opposing players. But two of the players had almost full range of motion. The years of playing rugby (which is tackle football without the protection of shoulder and hip pads) had taken no toll on them. This advantage enabled them to perform in rowing far beyond what their other, stiffer teammates could do. At an indoor rowing championship, when pitted against college athletes who had be rowing for 6-8 years, one of these rugby players won the open championship, and the other won the senior championship.

Both of these rowers had only been rowing for four months!

(A collegiate rower we later worked with went from #9 to #2 on his team in his ergometer score ((rowing on a stationary rowing machine)) after we released microfibers in his rib cage so that he could take in more oxygen. This shows you how much microfibers affect athletic performance of every kind.)

Athletes who form very few microfibers in response to injury, overuse, illness or tension, are few and far between. They tend to gravitate to activities that require a lot of flexibility, such as golf, martial arts, gymnastics and swimming. They are often the best in their chosen sport. If you look at the money list in golf, you see the golfers at the top are usually the most flexible. If you look at the bottom of the money list, you see golfers who are stiff.

The golfer with the most PGA tour wins is also the most flexible golfer of all time. Even in his seventies, he was able to kick his cleats up over his head into the top of a doorframe.

The problem is that you cannot tell if you are going to be one of those who will form microfibers, or one of the lucky, rare ones who will form them only minimally. Since it takes a year or two for microfibers to accumulate to the point where you can notice a loss of flexibility, by the time you notice the damage, it is already too late. Chances are very good that you will, since we find that athletes with full range of motion are very rare. For instance, we have measured hundreds of elite swimmers over the past 20 years and have found only one with all the minimum ranges of motion she needed for her stroke. She also set a World Record at age 16 that lasted twenty years! We have never found another athlete, in any sport, who had all the minimum ranges of motion for unimpeded movement in their sport. Especially golf, which requires more flexibility than any other sport, except swimming breaststroke.

This means that all the athletes that we have worked with over the past 35 years (and some of them were young swimmers, only ten years old) had microfibers in one or more ranges that were critical to their sport.

This is why some golfers can lift weights and still perform at a very high level, and actually seem to perform better after they have bulked up. But these athletes are very rare. All the professional golfers we have worked with had developed microfibers from lifting weights that were adversely affecting their game. Most of our work with them was undoing the damage caused by lifting weights and running.

Golfers do not lift weights to improve their putting. They lift weights to increase the length of their drives, and to get their ball out of tall rough. But lifting weights is not the only way to increase club head speed. By becoming more efficient, you can increase your club head speed and add yardage. By hitting the ball straighter, you can avoid the long rough.

Even if the best male and female golfers in the world have benefited from lifting weights, it does not mean that is the only way to improve, or that it will benefit your game as well. They are blessed in that they form very few microfibers, or form them very slowly. Eventually, they will lose flexibility, as everyone does, from the accumulation of microfibers. Everyone else will start to lose flexibility in a year or two.

Loss of flexibility will degrade every part of your game.

The length of your driver and fairway woods.

The accuracy of your irons, wedges and putter.

The comfort of your neck, shoulders, hips and lower back.

Restriction

Most of the work golfers do on the course is overcoming their own stiffness. It is not the narrowness and length of the fairways, the size and placement of the hazards, the wind, the heat, the pin placements, or the slope of the greens that are the toughest challenges in golf. The biggest challenge on any course is the stiffness of the golfers who are playing it.

This stiffness is not 'natural', just because almost everyone has it. It is a result of an over-reaction of the connective tissue. Connective tissue over-reacts to any insult or injury. You may still have scars on your knees or elbows from a fall you had in sixth grade. Is it really necessary to have that scar? Is it necessary or helpful for a scar to last for 40 years? Not at all. It is just an over-reaction of your connective tissue.

Microfibers are another form of scar tissue. Nature figured out how to put a cast around an area so that it could heal. It just never figured out how to remove it after healing had taken place. We are all walking around with a cast on. It is on the inside where we cannot see it. It allows some movement, but not freedom of movement.

Hidden Cost of Conventional Strength Training

The problem with lifting weights, 'core' work, sit-ups, push-ups, pull-ups, and running is that we initially feel better. We may even see an improvement in our game. But unless you are one in a million, you will eventually have to pay the piper. In a year or so, you will start to lose flexibility. It will be so gradual, that you will not notice it. The first sign is that you start to plateau. You are not improving as you originally had. Then you might start to notice a decline. It will be gradual. You may, as most golfers do, blame it on 'lack of concentration'. Or you may start hunting around for new clubs, a new teacher, a new swing thought. It won't occur to you that you have lost flexibility unless you measure your ranges. You can't tell by feel. We have found that golfers are usually unaware of **any** loss of flexibility until they have lost at least half the flexibility that they need for golf.

Once you have developed microfibers, you cannot stretch them out. This suggests another way another way to discover whether or not you have developed microfibers. Since stiffness in any area of your body is a sum of the tension in your muscles and the microfibers in your connective tissue, try stretching those areas that are stiff. If the problem is just tension, you will be able to achieve the minimum ranges (110° Trunk and Neck Rotation, 90° Arm Flexion, 60° Internal Hip Rotation) you need for golf.

If stretching does not get you to these minimums, you have developed microfibers.

To Know Your Flexibility, You Have to Measure

Measure. Measure. Measure. It is the only way to discover if you have microfibers that are undermining your golf game. Microfibers are too small to be seen on X-rays, MRI's or CT scans. You cannot feel them, although muscles that are bound up with microfibers feel harder than muscles that are free of them. If you have not done a lot of biceps curls, pull-ups or push-ups, your biceps are likely to be free of microfibers. An easy way to tell is to extend your elbow. If it opens up 180 degrees, you have full range of motion in that joint. Bend your elbow 90 degrees with your forearm resting on something so that your biceps are relaxed. Feel them with your fingers. They should be soft. All of your muscles should be this soft. If they are not, they are full of tension or surrounded by microfibers, or both.

Muscle Tone

We were surprised to find so much muscle softness when we started working with Olympic athletes. Like most people, we assumed that Olympic athletes would have lots of 'muscle tone'. But they don't. Tone is tension. Tense athletes are not successful. Cats don't have muscle tone. Dogs have muscle tone. Cats are much better athletes than dogs.

The reason that 'muscle tone' is bad for athletes is that muscles work in pairs—agonist (contracting muscle) and antagonist (stretching muscle). Research has shown that the antagonist is responsible for modulating the contraction of the agonist. If the antagonist does not readily stretch, or let go, the agonist cannot successfully contract. This is called inhibition of contraction. When you are swinging a club, you do not want your antagonists to inhibit the contraction of your agonists. This is how you lose clubhead speed.

When you putt, you want your muscles to contract freely. Any inhibition will affect the path of your putter head, as well as the square ness of the face at contact. In conventional putting, where you rely on your muscles for putter head speed, it will also affect the distance of your putt. Golfers, who short-putt under pressure, do so because they have contracted their antagonists. It's not that they don't contract their agonist muscles (the ones that swing the putter toward the target) enough, but that they are also contracting their opposing (antagonist) muscles.

If your antagonists are tight because of microfibers, they will also interfere with your swing and putting. It does not matter if it is tension or microfibers, tightness in your antagonists will literally hold you back on the golf course.

Low Back Pain

Microfibers are also responsible for the back problems that plague golfers, as we described in Chapter Eleven (Low Back Pain). But the microfibers are not in the lower back; they are surrounding the muscles of the hips and middle back. One of the few areas that has freedom of movement in golfers is the lower back. It feels stiff because the tension varies from day to day. But the stiffness of the hips and middle back is constant because so many microfibers develop in these two areas. Falls on our rear end and getting the wind knocked out of us are the two major causes.

Stiffness and Awareness

We tend not to notice areas of our body that don't move. They fade into the background. We experience pain and stiffness in our lower back because it pays the price for loss of flexibility in the middle back and hips. We find the hips and middle back rarely hurt. Most golfers think that where there is no pain, there is no problem. Nothing could be further from the truth. This is why you need to measure your ranges. Only measurement will tell you where you have lost flexibility. You cannot tell by feel. Areas that feel stiff are often more flexible that areas that are really tight because tension masks sensation.

As we said before, tension causes microfibers to form. When we fall on our read end as a kid, we tense up our muscles to deaden the pain. That tension initiated the formation of microfibers. The microfibers accumulate over time, so that by the time we are in our twenties or beyond, we have lost internal hip rotation. But the microfibers have done more than just accumulate (as bad as that is for us). They have also bound the original tension into place. The tension continues to mask sensation in our hips, including the sensation of stiffness. Our golfers are always shocked when they see just how much flexibility they have lost. While golfers need a minimum of 60 degrees of internal hip rotation, it is not uncommon to find golfers with only 20 or 30 degrees of motion. The tension in their hip muscles masks their loss of range.

Microfiber Reduction is Unique

As you know, microfibers can be released with Microfiber Reduction, our special form of connective tissue massage. There are many therapists who claim to release 'adhesions' in the connective tissue. We have worked with many golfers who have been to such therapists. They report that Microfiber Reduction is not only more effective, but also longer lasting.

Our clients have been told that saline injection, skin rolling, adjustments, cellulite machines, and electrical stimulation can release microfibers. None of this is true.

You Play Golf With Your Body

As one of our golfers so astutely said:

"You play golf with your body. If you want to change your game, you have to change your body."

CHAPTER THIRTEEN

Case Histories

Tony Rigas

Tony Rigas came to Somax in 2005 after spending many fruitless years trying to improve his golf game working with a well-known instructor. Tony was not able to improve with conventional instruction because his swing problems were caused by microfibers that had accumulated in the connective tissues between his muscles as a result of injuries and lifting weights. Conventional golf instruction does not release microfibers. As we released his microfibers with Microfiber Reduction, Tony was able to get his game on track.

Hip Abduction Range

Hip Abduction is critical for beginning the downswing with the left knee. We find that golfers have difficulty with this movement until their Hip Abduction Range reaches $90°$.

Tony was able to triple his Hip Abduction Range.

Before **After**

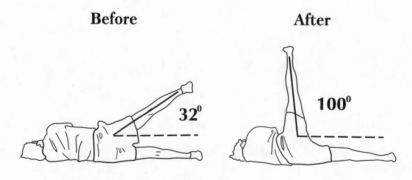

$32°$ $100°$

External Hip Rotation

When you rotate your hips away from the ball 60⁰, your right hip rotates 60⁰ internally, and your left hip rotates 60⁰ externally. If you do not have 60⁰ of External Hip Rotation, your own stiffness will impede an efficient backswing.

When your hips are 60⁰ open at impact, your left hip is rotated 60⁰ internally, while your right hip is rotated 60⁰ externally. If you do not have 60⁰ of External Hip Rotation on your right hip, your own stiffness will slow down the speed of your hips prior to impact.

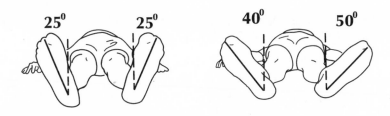

Internal Hip Rotation

Lack of Internal Hip Rotation is the single greatest cause of low back pain in golfers. As we increased Tony's Internal Hip Rotation, his chronic low back pain faded away.

In addition, Tony was able to rotate his hips away from the ball with less effort, which improved the length and accuracy of his drives.

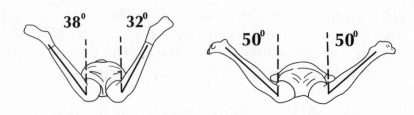

Neck Rotation

You need Neck Rotation in golf for two reasons.

The first is to be able to keep both eyes on the ball at the top of your backswing. If your neck is stiff, you will not be able to turn your shoulders 120° away from the ball, and yet keep both eyes on the ball. If you cannot turn your head enough, the bridge of your nose will cover up your right eye.

The second reason is that neck flexibility is critical for good putting. The head must remain perfectly still during the putt, as even a small amount of head movement will pull your eyes off the ball and you will have problems with good ball contact.

Tony was already an excellent putter before coming to Somax. But his lack of flexibility in his neck and trunk meant that he had to strain all his muscles in order to maintain good form. As you can see, Tony was able to more than double his Neck Rotation Range with Microfiber Reduction. Tony was then able to relax and enjoy putting.

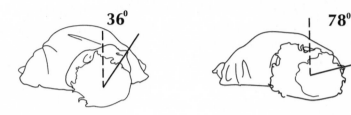

Trunk Rotation

Trunk Rotation is one of the keys to driving distance. Tony increased his average drive from 280 to over 300 yards.

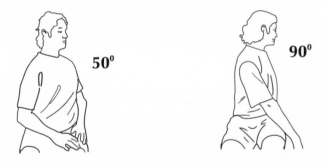

Tony wrote an eloquent and moving letter about the results of his experience at Somax.

When I first contacted you about your program to improve flexibility and reduce stiffness, I was very skeptical about the possible results and any lasting relief.

After years of lifting weights, running, injuries and stress at work, I felt stiff and old at 34. I was suffering from a tremendous amount of back pain before I came to see you. On a scale of one to ten, I was often at 7 or 8 and sometimes 10. There were times when I could not get up and walk around for several days.

I am a lifelong golfer, playing junior, high school, college and mini tour tournaments. At 6'5", I have had many years of stiffness and pain in my back and hips. I have seen scores of massage therapists, personal trainers, physical therapists, chiropractors and acupuncturists; all who had promised to ease the stiffness and reduce the pain. Despite the years of effort I put into physical therapy and stretching, not to mention taking prescription non-steroidal anti-inflammatory drugs, I was not seeing any lasting improvements.

In order to play golf regularly, I had to get weekly massages and see a chiropractor 2 to 3 times a week. The pain and stiffness were still there soon after the treatments. Frustration and depression about the pain had been setting in for quite awhile. So it should come as no surprise that I had reservations about another form of treatment.

I was extremely flexible as a teenager and still had this image of myself being very flexible. When you initially measured my flexibility ranges, I was shocked at how much flexibility I had lost. I never dreamed that my ranges of motion were now so limited. Having seen pictures of people that you worked with, and how flexible they became, I was cautiously hopeful.

When you worked with me I saw results so quickly, it was mind blowing! I was so excited to find something that worked and didn't go away after a day or two like a massage or chiropractic adjustment. My flexibility came back almost instantly along with a large reduction in pain. I actually could not believe how much flexibility I had lost in my body and even more impressive is that it could be restored! I wouldn't have to go on living and hurting like this. The most amazing aspect was that the results lasted! Now, a year later, I'm still amazed.

I also saw great improvements in my golf game. The first time I went out and played golf after seeing you, I shot a 67, five under par! I was so relaxed and carefree that I felt like I was 16 years old again. Before I saw you I was struggling for accuracy with my driver, hitting it 280 yards or so. Now, my drives are less erratic and I am able to get a bigger shoulder and hip turn, hitting my driver consistently 300 yards or more, with less effort. I have also had to recalibrate how far I hit my irons, picking up an additional 10 to 15 yards per club.

Putting has become much easier as well. I was putting well statistically before I saw you, averaging 29 putts per round. However, this came at a great personal expense. In tournaments, I would find my stomach in knots and my neck/head and forearms were shaking over putts. So, even though the ball went in the hole, it wasn't much fun.

I was always trying to make an arc with my stroke and take my hands "out" of my stroke, with little success. I would practice for hours, but once I got on the course I couldn't do it and reverted to a straight back and through method using my hands & forearms. Now, I am able to keep my head still and let my body stroke the putt, and have an arc to my stroke. This has led to a much better roll on the ball. I like to draw a line on my ball to line up my putts. I noticed that when I would putt before I saw you that the ball might go in the hole but it was skidding or the line was wobbling. Now, the ball rolls pure – end over end. It's so much easier and smoother, when I get going on the practice green, I'll make ten 6 to 8 footers in a row without even lining it up!

Having taken lessons from a famous golf instructor for years was a waste of time and money. I just couldn't put my body in the positions he wanted, or move like he instructed. It was not a lack of effort either. At times I was hitting balls for 7 hours/ day and still not making progress! I started believing that it was talent or some gift that let other people swing or move a certain way.

Of course, now it makes perfect sense that lacking flexibility will negatively affect my golf swing. Since I wasn't able to turn my hips, I would have to make some kind of compensation in my swing. I didn't make this connection until I saw you.

You definitely gave me more than I expected with your program. My swing technique got drastically better and my stress and tension levels have come down tremendously. Feeling better on the golf course is one thing, but even more impressive are the changes in my personal life. My wife says that I am a totally different person now (for the better) than I was a year ago. I'm handling problems with greater ease and confidence and have a more relaxed disposition. It is amazing how much your entire life can be impacted from tension and pain!

I would highly recommend your program to anyone wanting to improve their athletic performance or suffering from tightness, stiffness or pain. As well as, anyone who is looking to reduce their stress & tension levels. I look forward to working with you further and becoming even more flexible and relaxed.

Thank you for all your help and ongoing support.

Best Regards,

Tony Rigas

Miriam Nagl

LPGA Touring professional Miriam Nagl started working with Somax at the end of July 2004 after experiencing severe back pain as a result of extensive weight lifting. During the course of her program at Somax, Miriam began working with our Power Hip Trainer, which has since become a consistent tool in her training regimen.

As Miriam became more flexible through our Microfiber Reduction program, she realized how stretching had not helped her to turn the way she wanted to. The pictures below show just some of the improvements in her flexibility through her Somax program.

Hip Abduction Range

Miriam increased her Hip Abduction Range 654% with Microfiber Reduction. As her Hip Abduction improved, it became easier to start her downswing with her left knee.

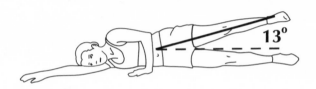

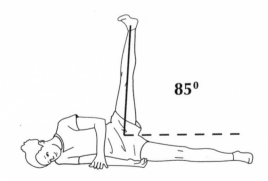

Hip Extension Range

Hip Extension is critical to an efficient golf swing, as the left hip is extended at the top of the backswing, and the right hip is extended at the finish.

Miriam doubled her Hip Extension with Microfiber Reduction.

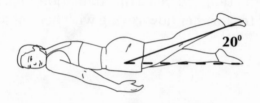

Arm Flexion Range

Golfers need a minimum of 90⁰ of Arm Flexion to get their Arm Angle on their backswing to 90⁰. Miriam increased her Arm Flexion 50% with Microfiber Reduction.

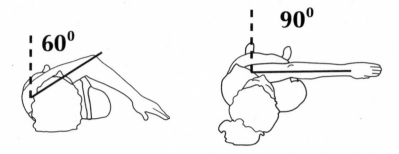

Trunk Rotation

Miriam almost doubled her Trunk Rotation with Microfiber Reduction.

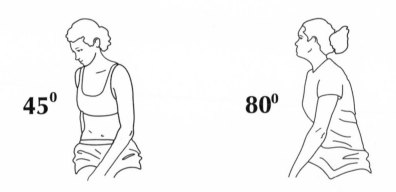

How did a 24 year-old female golfer lose so much flexibility? With lots of hard work. Since age 14, Miriam was on an intense physical training program, including lifting weights and lots of 'core' work. The result was that overusing her muscles in this way created microfibers, a mild form of scar tissue, which bound her muscles together. Once formed, these microfibers accumulated over time, making her stiffer as she got older.

Most of the work we have done with professional golfers has been undoing the damage caused by 'core' work, lifting weights and running. Miriam did all three.

Here are the results of her Somax program in her swing mechanics.

Address and Backswing Down the Line

With her added flexibility from Microfiber Reduction, Miriam felt comfortable standing more erect at address, was able to keep her hands and club more on plane during her backswing, and could get her club and hands exactly on plane at the top of her backswing. Stiffness in her shoulders and trunk made it impossible to get on plane before. By releasing microfibers that were binding her muscles together, Somax made it possible for her to attain the efficient swing positions she wanted.

Before   **After**

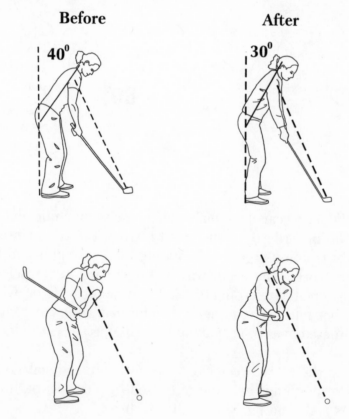

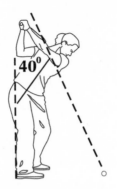 

Downswing, Impact and Follow Through Down the Line

After Microfiber Reduction, Miriam's downswing was more on plane; her Spine Angle at impact was exactly the same as at address (instead of the 7° difference before) and her follow-through was more on plane. Maintaining a constant Spine Angle and staying on plane are the keys to good ballstriking.

Microfiber Reduction also freed up her hips, allowing her to turn them faster, as you can see below: her hips are more open at impact.

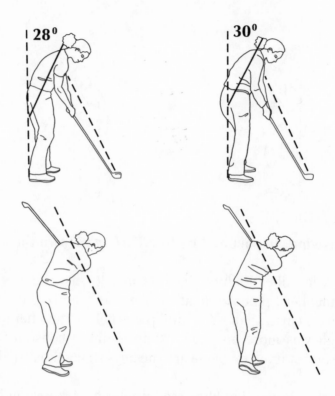

Address and Backswing from the Front

After Microfiber Reduction, Miriam's spine is more vertical at address, and she was able to get her left Arm Angle to 82° above horizontal at the top of her backswing, as compared to just 47° before her Somax program. Her Shoulder Turn Angle increased from 115° to 142°.

The modern convention is to restrict the Arm Angle and Shoulder Turn Angle, but this is just because most golfers are so stiff. Golfers with a restricted turn have to use enormous muscular effort to achieve a decent club head speed. This increases the stress on the body, resulting in chronic back, neck and shoulder pain.

Flexible golfers can make a 120°+ shoulder turn and strike the ball well. A golfer with a 142⁰ Shoulder Turn Angle won more PGA tournaments that any other golfer in history.

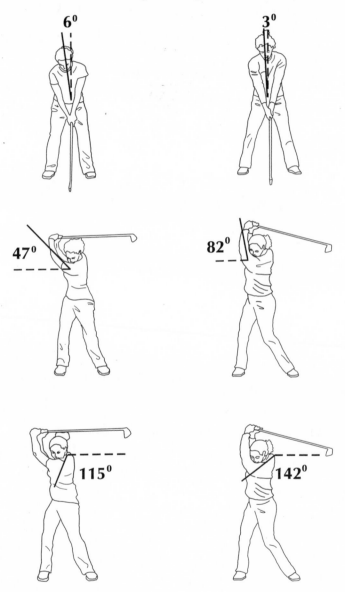

Downswing, Impact and Follow Through from the Front

Improving Arm Flexion and the Arm Angle in golfers usually eliminates any casting, as you can see in the photos below. Miriam has eliminated a 20^0 cast on her downswing, which increased her club head speed and the length of her drives.

Before her Somax program, Miriam's Front Spine Angle tripled from 6^0 to 18^0! Sliding her hips instead of turning them caused this huge increase in spine tilt to her right. Golfers with stiff hips always find it easier to slide rather than turn. After her Somax program, Miriam's Front Spine Angle at Impact (FSAI) was only 4^0 greater than her Front Spine Angle at Address (FSAA).

As we have noted before, increasing your Front Spine Angle opens your clubface at impact. Golfers try to correct for this by turning the clubface over with their hands. Sometimes it works, sometimes it doesn't, and sometimes you hook the ball. This was the problem that Miriam had before her Somax program--her balls were going right and left. After her Somax program, she was hitting the ball straighter than ever before.

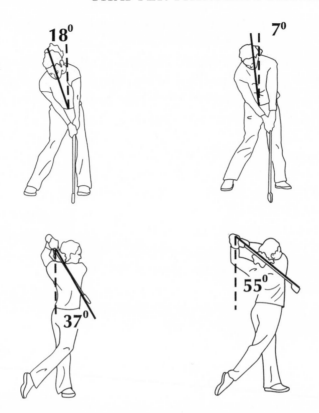

The results of her Somax program showed up in Miriam's earnings. In 2004 she made $38,000 in tour earnings. In 2005, she made $152,000. She quadrupled her earnings in one year.

Miriam also won her first tournament in two years after her Somax program. She won the Euro Q-school tournament with a 72-71-71-71. Not a bad score for a golfer who had problems with consistency.

Miriam made an insightful comment while explaining her reason for choosing to work with Somax.

"You play golf with your body. If you want to change your game, you have to change your body."

Here is her report of her experience:

Before I started working with Somax, I only knew one thing: lifting weights would change my body and therefore help me improve my performance. What I didn't know was that the muscles, although getting stronger, were also becoming glued together with microfibers.

In the summer of 2004, I was experiencing severe back pain and discomfort around my hips from weight lifting. This pain began to impact my performance as a professional golfer. I started doing Yoga, went to see different massage therapists and changed my workout routine to get some relief. Yet nothing seemed to ease the pain.

I noticed during my stretching sessions (which would sometimes last 1 1/2 hours) that many of my muscles just wouldn't give. I would feel good for the next 4 hours, but by the time I cooled down the pain had returned. I also noticed very little improvement in flexibility from one session to another.

I remember how frustrating that time was for me. During all the years of strength training and stretching, the various coaches that I worked with only taught me about the muscles. Never did anybody mention the connective tissue that surrounds them and what could go wrong with it.

When I first saw the demonstration tape of Microfiber Reduction, I was skeptical that this procedure would really help my problems.

I am now into my second year of working with Somax and I couldn't be happier about the results that I have seen from their work with me. They have enabled me to work on my game with no pain in my body. They have improved my flexibility in areas I didn't even know were of any importance to golf.

I have never seen a program that is as individualized as this one and that carries as many benefits.

I have improved all of my statistics on Tour by becoming more flexible and tension free.

One example of the benefits this program has given me is visible improvement in my putting. My head used to move a lot during my stroke. I would work on it for hours with little result. After the first year of my Somax program, I have improved my LPGA putting statistics from 1.86 (T 112) in 2004 to 1.81 (T 27) in 2005 (Putts per Green in Regulation) and my head movement has decreased dramatically.

I have also quadrupled my income as a player, and won my first tournament in two years, both of which have made me very happy.

As Somax got rid of the microfibers between my muscles, it enabled me to move the way I know I should move. This is partly what has increased my level of confidence as an athlete.

Tension Reduction is another bonus of the program. I noticed that my focus and concentration levels have improved by releasing tension. Nowadays, I feel much more relaxed on and off the golf course. Situations where I felt pressure in the past don't seem to bother me anymore.

The biggest lesson I have learned from working with Somax is that scar tissue around our muscles just doesn't let us perform to our capabilities. Once this scar tissue is released, there is no limit to our performance and well-being!

Thank You Somax.

Miriam Nagl

LPGA and Euro Tour

Dan Henrichs

Backswing

These drawings show Dan Henrichs' backswing before and after his Somax program, which he finished in October 2000 at age 55. Dan increased his Arm Angle from 27° to 45° after we released microfibers in his left shoulder with Microfiber Reduction. We also released microfibers in his back, which allowed him to increase his Shoulder Turn Angle from 90⁰ to 120⁰.

As a result, Dan can bring his club shaft closer to horizontal. He has improved his Backswing Angle from -30° to -2°. With his larger, more flexible turn, Dan was able to hit one club longer with his irons, and increased the distance of his drives from 235 to 250, with more drives hitting the fairway.

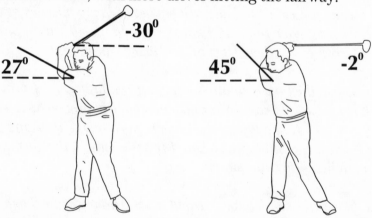

Cast Angle

These drawings show the improvement in Dan's Cast Angle. Prior to Somax, Dan cast his club 45°. After we released the microfibers in his shoulders and back, he has eliminated casting his club. He was able to rotate his hips 30° more open at his Cast Point, as they are were longer restricted with microfibers. Before coming to Somax, his shoulders and hips moved as one unit because of the microfibers in his back. Afterwards, he was able to separate the two, rotating his hips ahead of his shoulders, creating a more powerful downswing.

Finish Angle

These drawings show the improvement in Dan's Finish Angle. Dan increased his Finish Angle from -3° to +55°. Combined with the 28° improvement in his Backswing Angle, Dan has increased the total range of his club shaft by 80°. The increased Finish Angle is more than cosmetic. Golfers with a small Finish Angle actually have to slow their club head down before impact. With his increased flexibility, Dan was able to increase his club head speed and distance for all his clubs. Dan's additional flexibility also greatly reduced his back pain while playing golf.

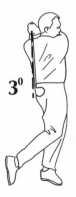 

Another benefit of Microfiber Reduction is apparent from these drawings. Dan is taller and thinner. Microfibers released from around his rib cage allowed him to expand his chest and lengthen his trunk. Before his Somax program, Dan's chest expanded only 1" when he took a deep breath. Afterwards it expanded 4". His breathing was easier and fuller twenty-four hours a day.

Dan writes:

I am definitely striking the ball better with more consistency. Since starting to play regularly again, I am really showing improvement. This last weekend, I went to Chicago to see my son and to play a round of golf. He was very impressed with my new golf swing. He has never seen me strike the ball better. In the past I could occasionally hit the ball fairly long, but I was inconsistent, because I came so far out of position when I took a hard swing at the ball. It took a lot of practice just to be able to hit the ball at all. I am especially happy to not to dip at the ball on the down swing. As you know, we worked on that problem for quite a while before finally putting it to rest.

Today I consistently hit at least one club longer with my irons. My driving is now regularly farther. Before my Somax program, I was driving 235 yards, but it was hard to keep it in the fairway. Now I consistently hit the ball over 250 yards with pretty good accuracy. I do occasionally hit the ball 300 yards. When I am not hitting the ball as good as I know that I can, I just go back to the basics we worked on and can begin hitting the ball solidly, with accuracy, fairly quickly.

*When I first came to Somax I was having serious lower back problems. They had become so severe that I was suffering with pains down my leg that were affecting my quality of life significantly. I was taking **four** 200mg ibuprofen tablets at a dose every **four** hours during the day in an effort to cope with the pain. When I played golf it would irritate my back significantly* *and would literally put me on the floor in pain. My pain began to subside as more and more parts of my body were loosened up with the Microfiber Reduction. Today I seldom have any pain in my lower back and virtually none running down my leg. My quality of life has improved significantly and I attribute this all to the Somax program.*

The most amazing thing is that I have not had any loss of flexibility since I have finished my program. I still stretch on a regular basis, but the flexibility is there even before I stretch. The process is also so sudden in the manner in which it works. As soon as the microfibers are released, that area just loosens up right away and has stayed loose.

During the first phase of the program we worked upon my breathing and chest expansion. This was quite remarkable and, to be frank, was definitely not something I was even concerned about. As it turns out, I was only expanding my diaphragm area one inch before the Microfiber Reduction. The expansion is now over four inches. This difference helps me sleep more soundly and I just feel more alive all during the day.

I went to Somax to improve my ability to play golf. It has actually worked out that the other benefits are far more important to me than being able to strike the ball better than I ever have in the past.

Richard Troxel

Backswing

These drawings show Dick Troxel's backswing before and after his Somax program, which he completed at age 68. Dick increased his Arm Angle from 20° to 35° after we released microfibers in his left shoulder with Microfiber Reduction. As a result, Dick can bring his club shaft closer to horizontal. He has improved his Backswing Angle from -15° to -10°. If you look at the distribution of his weight around the vertical broken line, you can see he had a reverse pivot at the top of his backswing because of tightness in his hips. After releasing the microfibers in his hips, Dick was able to rotate away from the ball while keeping his weight evenly divided between both legs.

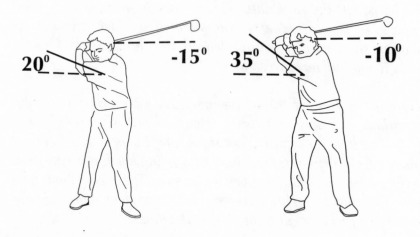

20° **-15°** **35°** **-10°**

Cast Angle

These drawings show the improvement in Dick's Cast Angle. Prior to Somax, Dick cast his club 30°. After releasing the microfibers in his shoulders and back, his Cast Angle is now just 10°.

Dick also now rotates his hips rather than sliding them to his left, as they are no longer restricted with microfibers. Before coming to Somax, Dick would shift his hips to his left in an attempt to get some club head speed. This is a common strategy in golfers who do not have much Internal Hip Rotation. After we released the microfibers in his hips, he was able to rotate his hips and keep his weight evenly distributed between his right and left legs prior to impact.

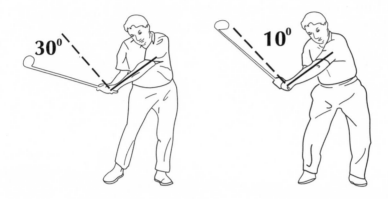

Finish

These drawings show the improvement in Dick's finish. Dick increased his Finish Angle from -25° to +15°. Combined with the 28° improvement in his Backswing Angle, Dick has increased the total range of his club shaft by 45°. The increased Finish Angle is more than cosmetic. Golfers with a small Finish Angle actually have to slow their club head down before impact. Dick's additional flexibility also greatly reduced his back pain during golf.

Another benefit of Microfiber Reduction is apparent from these drawings. Dick looks taller and thinner. Microfibers released from his rib cage allowed him to expand his chest and lengthen his trunk. Prior to his Somax program, his chest expanded only 1" when he took a deep breath. After his microfibers were released, his chest expanded 3". His lower chest (diaphragm) expansion increased from .5" to 2.5", a 500% improvement. Dick lost his breathing flexibility as a result of several bouts of pneumonia when he was very young.

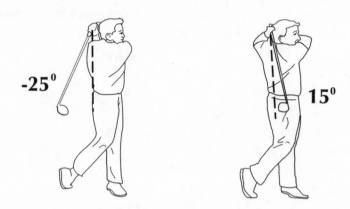

Dick writes:

A major objective in working with Somax was to develop flex-ibility to compensate for the polio experience I had as an in-fant. The inflexibility that is so evident in the "before" photos can, I believe, be related to the tightness (or microfibers) in my back and upper leg muscles that are (in my opinion) polio re-lated. There is no question in my mind that Microfiber Reduc-tion opened up flexibility that never before had been available to me.

Golf really is only a secondary benefit that I achieved from our work. The items cited in the final paragraph are, to me, much more important benefits of Microfiber Reduction. My wife points out that my back is straighter and I stand taller. (I had a "lump" of some sort in my upper spine that was eliminated during our first few sessions together.) I can, for example, walk longer distances without panting and am less tired while travel-ing, golfing or other activities. My golf swing is, as the pictures demonstrate, more complete. To me, these changes are more sig-nificant than being able to hit a longer tee shot.

Less obvious: I now have an early morning, daily workout at our club gym, including bike riding and stretching. I have joined health clubs in the past but NEVER stuck with the regimen. No doubt the Microfiber Reduction has somehow given me the confidence/motivation to realize that aerobic exercise is truly beneficial.

Another point that is relevant is how quickly these changes were accomplished. The improved turn etc. occurred within minutes after removing microfibers. It did not require additional weeks of stretching and gym work. Indeed, it is unlikely that any such gym work could have produced these changes.

I recently spent a golfing weekend with an old friend who is my age. He walked in a bent-over posture and could hit the ball maybe 75% as far as my drives. I have no doubt that without Microfiber Reduction that would be me. I showed the pictures to a friend who is a former club professional and he said he was most impressed with the change in my leg action in the "before" and "after" pictures.

CHAPTER FOURTEEN

Help!

If you run into any problems improving your swing and putting mechanics, you can get help:

1. By phone—there is a one-hour minimum; we can discuss whatever problems you are experiencing while trying to improve your efficiency in golf. You can also send us videotapes of your swing, which we can download, analyze and measure, and then email you our analysis. Call 800-227-6629 to schedule an appointment

2. DVD's—all the methods covered in this book are in our DVD **The Efficient Golfer**. You can watch us measuring a golfer's mechanics, flexibility and strength and making improvements in their swing and putt.. You can learn how to stretch four core ranges with our **Are You Flexible Enough for Golf?** DVD. You can learn how to measure and stretch your breathing ranges with our **Breathing** DVD. The DVD's can be ordered through the Somax Sports website at w**ww.somaxsports.com**

3. Camps—our golf camps are five days. We videotape everyone's swing and putt from the front and down the line and measure their mechanics. Participants learn to measure each other's four core ranges and test strength in trunk and hip rotation. You then learn how to go about improving your Range, Sequence, Separation, Speed and Alignment (RSSSA). You will be able to try out our Pendulum Putters, Hip Speedometers and Power Hip Trainers. The camp schedule, description and fees can be found at **www.somaxsports.com**

4. Evaluation—you can schedule a three-hour individual evaluation at our center. We will videotape your swing and putt, measure your swing mechanics and flexibility, test your strength, improve your flexibility with Microfiber Reduction, and re-tape your swing. You will see an improvement right away. Call 800-227-6629 to schedule.

5. Microfiber Reduction—improving your flexibility in all 44 ranges for golf will enable you to swing the club with less strain and effort, as well as improving the accuracy of all of your clubs and putter. A program of Microfiber Reduction is minimum of 1-6 weeks, which can be done over any period of time. Please order our demo tape package so that you can measure your ranges and see an example of Microfiber Reduction. The package is $20, which is refundable with any program. To order, call 800-227-6629.

6. Stress Reduction—a program that utilizes acupressure points to reduce stress and overcome old habits. The program is taught in one two-hour phone session, and after that you will be able apply it to any type of stress on your own. Call 800-227-6629 to schedule an appointment.

CHAPTER FIFTEEN

Equipment and Training Aids

You cannot achieve efficient putting and swing mechanics with conventional putters and training aids. We recommend the following:

1. Somax Power Hip Trainer—the only aerobic exercise machine that increases the strength and speed of hip rotation for golf. Available at the Somax Sports web-site **www.somaxsports.com**

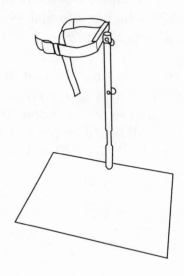

2. Somax Pendulum Putting System--- a shorter, more upright putter so that you can putt with your arms hanging down relaxed, instead of sucking your arms into your stomach as you have to do with conventional putters. The putter head is heavier (500 grams), which

encourages the use of the stomach muscles while putting. Also available at **www.somaxsports.com**

3. Somax Hip Speedometer—a pager-like device worn on the belt that measures your hip acceleration and deceleration. Since it can be worn while playing a round, it gives you invaluable feedback on how well you are rotating your hips. Available at **www.somaxsports.com**

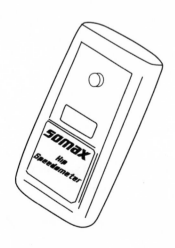

F.A.Q.'s

Aren't there golfers who are very successful with idiosyncratic, inefficient swings?

Yes, just as there are racecar drivers who can win races with cars that are less efficient than their competitors! But in car racing, millions are spent every year perfecting racecars, so race teams have put their money on efficiency, as should you.

The golf equivalent to the racecar is the human body. Clubs and balls are just the wheels and tires of golf. Wheels and tires are important, but they won't win a race on a car full of rust (microfibers) and a squirrelly suspension (poor swing mechanics).

If golfers want to improve their game, they need to improve their engine (range, sequence, separation and hip speed) and suspension (alignment).

You wouldn't drive a car where the front wheels wobbled (alignment problems) or the drive train and crankshaft were rusted (microfibers), would you?

As one of our pros said so eloquently, "You play golf with your body. If you want to change your game, you have to change your body."

If every golfer adopted your ideas, won't they all have identical, mechanical, boring swings? Where is there room for individuality?

1. Golfers will have similar swings, providing they have sufficient flexibility, once they realize the value of efficiency.

2. Formula One, Indy and NASCAR cars all look pretty much alike, because there is only one most efficient design for any engineering problem (in this case, getting around the track or course in the least amount of time). New designs will emerge as innovations are made, but racecars are much more uniform than they were 50 years ago.

3. Racing is no less interesting than it was 50 years ago. In fact, the number of fans has increased dramatically as the cars have become faster.

4. As golfers become more efficient, scores will go down, competition will be more intense, more golfers will hole out from the fairway, and you will see more holes in one. I don't see baseball fans bored by homeruns. Do you think golf fans will bored by eagles?

5. Golfers are funny. They praise a goofy swing by saying 'it gets the job done'. But they wouldn't buy a car where the front wheels wobbled (poor Alignment); the engine had blow-by and spewed smoke all over the place and could barely chug up the hill (poor Sequence, Separation and Speed), or the bearings were frozen (poor Range).

6. Is our individuality wrapped up in our failings? Do we have to have to be stiff to be an individual? Do we have to have problems keeping our club on plane to be human? What about our accomplishments? Don't they count for anything? No pride to be found in a 280-yard drive that splits the fairway? How about sinking a 20-foot birdie putt?

Isn't re-engineering a golfer just a fancy term for stretching?

1. First of all, increasing the flexibility of a club shaft is re-engineering. You make physical changes in the materials of the club shaft in order to change the way it behaves during the swing. While stretching does make some minor improvement in flexibility, most of them are in 'how you feel'. When you measure the actual number of degrees you can increase your internal hip rotation, trunk rotation or arm flexion with conventional stretches, the improvements are minimal. This does not mean it is a waste of time to 'loosen up' before you swing, but you are not re-engineering your body when you do so.

2. Secondly, what materials in the body are you changing when you stretch? The answer is that you are not changing any materials—you are just lowering, temporarily, the level of tension in your muscles. Imagine if a club maker came out with a new club that 'temporarily' changed its flexibility, but had to be 'stretched' every day before you use it? Would anyone buy such a club? No, because it would be unreliable and require too much upkeep.

3. When microfibers and tension are released, they are gone for good. They are released so that the muscles can slide past each other easily, and not restrict the movement you have to go through for an efficient swing. It is a change in the infrastructure of the body (the connective tissue system) so that it can perform its function (facilitating the movement of the muscles). The result is a long-lasting and dramatic improvement in the body of the golfer.

4. Stretching, by the way, is the least effective way to im-

prove flexibility. It is a technology that is at least 2,000 years old. Yoga has been popular in India for millennia. If it was helpful to golf, there would be many successful Indian golfers, but this does not seem to be the case.

I know I am flexible, because I can touch my palms to the floor with my knees straight. How can Microfiber Reduction help someone who is already flexible?

We have worked with golfers who were able to put their palms on the floor with their knees straight, but had only 20⁰ of Internal Hip Rotation when we measured their flexibility.

You only know if you have enough flexibility for golf when you measure your golf ranges. Touching the floor with your palms is not one of them.

Don't you have to be a golfer to teach someone golf?

Do cardiologists have to have heart disease to help you? Do oncologists have to have cancer? Would you only hire a carpenter who built his own house? Would you insist that dress designers wear dresses?

Playing a sport and analyzing and improving it are two completely different talents.

Many of the elite and professional athletes we have worked with cannot tell us what they do, and are often surprised to see what they are actually doing, once they have a chance to review their videotapes with us.

We do not throw the javelin, but a javelin thrower won his only Gold Medal after we worked with him. We do not row, but a team of amateur rowers made the Olympic Trials in less than six months after they worked with us. We do not swim, but our swimmers have won 43 Gold Medals and set 11 World

Records. We do not run, but our runners cut a minute per mile off their running pace.

Sometimes it pays to be outside the field looking in. You have a better perspective as to what is going on. You are not confined by conventions. You are not blinded by conformity. You are not bound by un-spoken rules.

There is no guarantee that someone will shoot lower scores if they follow your advice, is there?

The only guarantee in life is that some day we will all pass away.

Our advice is four-fold:

1. If you follow the conventions of dropping the hands at address and shifting your weight prior to impact, you are making good ball contact more difficult than it has to be.

2. The biggest problem facing golfers is lack of flexibility in one or more of the 44 ranges of motion required for the golf swing and putt, even among junior golfers. Golfers are unaware of these restrictions, for the most part, because they do not measure their ranges, and they do not feel any loss of flexibility until they have lost at least half of the range they need.

3. The modern restricted swing increases the chances of injury because it requires muscular effort to replace Range in order to maintain clubhead speed. This effort over a restricted Range increases the stresses on your body. Increasing your flexibility so that you can take a full turn and utilize an efficient downswing sequence that starts with your left knee will reduce the chance of injury, reduce the effort of your swing, and increase

your consistency.

4. The conventional putting stance, grip, stroke and putter are not efficient.

I notice that some golfers who 'go ballistic' (let their arms and club extend) with their driver maintain their wrist angle with their irons. If you can do it, isn't it better to maintain your wrist angle with your irons?

Good question. Most golfers are more accurate with their irons not because the clubs are shorter, but because they maintain the same wrist angle at impact that they did at address. It is precisely for this reason that we recommend you address the ball with your hands on your swing plane for all your clubs,. In this way, you can 'go ballistic' on your downswing and still have excellent ball contact. Since you will not have to exert a lot of pressure to keep your wrist angle (it is already extended), you will reduce the number of microfibers you will develop in your forearms from using your driver and irons. This is a good thing.

What about the grip? Isn't that important?

Apart from the putter, we don't spend much time on the grip, because most of our clients are single-digit players or better. They all know how to grip the club.

If you are not sure, any competent pro can teach you how to grip the club.

There are even clubs with molded grips that will show you how to grip.

We go along with convention in this one matter, and recommend that you grip your clubs with the base of your fingers instead of the palms.

We don't have any opinions on weak, neutral or strong grips. The right grip is the one that squares up your clubface at impact.

The grip is not as important as what you are doing with your hips, spine and swing plane.

In golf, as in the rest of life, the tail does not wag the dog.

If your ideas are so good, why hasn't anyone come up with them before?

Actually, one professional golfer did place his hands on his swing plane at address, and he became a legendary ball-striker, capable of hitting over 1000 drives into a 30-yard circle in a single day.

As for Microfiber Reduction, Tension Reduction, STMR, RSSA, Rocket Theory of Golf, Power Hip Trainer, Hip Speedometer, and Pendulum Putting System—someone has to be the first, or else no discoveries would ever be made.

Golfers who have followed our ideas have been remarkably successful: #113 to #1 in tour putting average, winning the US Open, quadrupling tour income, increasing longest drive from 295 to 400, and eliminating low back pain.

Not a bad record.

I will never be able to do Microfiber Reduction. What can I do to improve my golf game?

It is not very useful to say 'never'. It would be more useful to say 'How can I do Microfiber Reduction'. In this way, you may be able to come up with a way to do it.

In the meantime, get a camcorder and tape your swing and putt from the front and down the line and analyze and measure what you are doing. If you are not sure how to do this, get an evaluation or do a Golf Camp.

Get your hands on your swing plane at address. Turn away from the ball as far as you can without changing your spine angles, and start your downswing with your left knee. Get our Pendulum Putting System and start using your stomach muscles for putting.

Alert your family and friends that the only birthday and holiday gift that you want is Microfiber Reduction.

I have tried deep tissue massage and it didn't last. How is Microfiber Reduction different?

This is a common complaint that we get from our clients who have tried conventional forms of deep tissue massage. After working with us, they report that the improvements are more dramatic and longer lasting.

I live in Timbuktu. How can I use your services?

We have sports engineers who travel. We can schedule your program wherever you live.

This new swing you propose looks so unnatural.

What was natural a century ago is not natural now. A century ago people rode horses, wore guns strapped to their hips, used outhouses, and mail communication could take months. Now we fly on planes, wear pagers, have sumptuous marble bathrooms and instant messaging. We feel a little sorry for the hardships people had to suffer a century ago, but do not feel any sorrow for the hardships golfers endure today using a century-old swing.

Think of the young pro with a family to support struggling on tour with a swing that is more than 100 years old. Does that sound appealing? Would he or she use clubs that were a century old? How about a century-old ball?

There is no law against addressing the ball with your hands on the swing plane, or improving your flexibility to the point where you can enjoy a full, effortless turn away from the ball, or starting your downswing with your left knee. It's only convention that keeps you from doing something new. It is convention and stiffness that rob you of an enjoyable morning or afternoon on a beautiful golf course, or a decent paycheck for your family.

Why is it so difficult to change my golf swing?

The biggest impediment to change is lack of flexibility. Most golfers have the most efficient swing that they can muster, given their current pattern of stiffness. Improve your flexibility and you can start to improve your swing right away.

My teaching pro (trainer, physical therapist, physician, golf buddies, parents) say that your book is all 'smoke and mirrors'. Who should I believe?

First of all, many people have problems with new ideas, especially if they perceive them as a threat to their profession or income.

Secondly, 'smoke and mirrors' is not a fact; it is an opinion, to which everyone is entitled. The question you have to ask yourself is this: am I going to live my life based on the opinions of others, or am I going to make my own decisions?

If you are in doubt about the wisdom of what we have to say, start by taking photos of your flexibility and swing and then measuring. If you have flexibility deficits and swing problems, start with our stretching video. If stretching does not improve your flexibility or swing mechanics, order our demo tape on Microfiber Reduction and send us your flexibility measurements. We can then discuss your options. If you like what you hear, schedule an evaluation, Golf Camp, or individual program.

When moving into a new realm, the best way is to take one small step at a time, rather than reject everything you see and hear.

We have used the same system of **RSSSA** and Microfiber Reduction to train swimmers, who have won 43 Gold Medals and set 11 World Records. We once sent some information on our program to the president of a swim team. Instead of making up his own mind, he passed the information along to his coach, who said it was all 'smoke and mirrors'. As a result, the president did not hire us to train his swim team. Six months later, the coach was let go when it was discovered he had been embezzling funds from the team.

We were invited to demonstrate our work to the head of research for a large training center. When we showed him the spectacular improvements in his athletes' flexibility with Microfiber Reduction, he said the results were 'not significant'. A year later he was let go when it was discovered that he had been falsifying research data in his publications.

We welcome criticism and differing opinions. But when you hear a blanket rejection, take it with a grain of salt.

My pro (trainer, physical therapist, etc.) says that only people who are double-jointed have as much flexibility as you recommend as the minimum you need for golf.

There is no such thing as 'double-jointed'. Some people may

have lax joints, such as the ability to hyper-extend their knees or elbows, but you don't need to do this to achieve 60^0 of internal hip rotation, 90^0 of arm flexion, and 110^0 of trunk and neck rotation. All you need to do is reduce the amount of tension in your muscles, and the number of microfibers in your connective tissue.

A number of golfers we have worked with actually had lax elbow and knee joints, but had very poor flexibility in the ranges they needed for golf. It demonstrated to us that flexibility is not a function of the joint itself, but of tension in the muscles, and microfibers in the connective tissue around the joint.

My strength trainer says that his clients actually improve their flexibility with weight training and has studies to prove it.

Until he can show you before and after photos, take this claim with a grain of salt. It's possible that there may be some initial, small improvement in flexibility with someone who was sedentary before lifting weights, as long as they move their joints through a full range while lifting.

But what happens a year or two later when microfibers have accumulated in the connective tissue around the muscles where you have torn muscle fibers? We know these microfibers form a cast around the muscles involved with lifting, because most of the work we have done with professional golfers was undoing the stiffness caused by lifting weights. As we released their microfibers, they recalled the soreness they felt from lifting weights.

What do you recommend for distance control?

We recommend the clock system. If you need to shorten the distance of your clubs, take your left arm back to 9, 10 or 11 o'clock instead of 12. You can also choke up on your grip.

Each inch you choke up on your grip will reduce your distance by about 10 yards. But always start your downswing with your left knee, making sure your Sequence is 1-5.

I have tried a heavier putter, but my putting has not improved.

Have you videotaped your spine from the back with your shirt off? If your spine is restricted, it is unrealistic to expect an improvement in your putting. It would be like expecting a car with a frozen drive shaft to go faster by installing heavier wheels.